CONTRADICTION SET FREE

Also Available from Bloomsbury

Aesthetic Theory, Theodor W. Adorno
Heine and Critical Theory, Willi Goetschel
Critical Theory and the Critique of Political Economy: On Subversion and Negative Reason, Werner Bonefeld
Critical Theory and the Crisis of Contemporary Capitalism, Heiko Feldner and Fabio Vighi

CONTRADICTION SET FREE

Hermann Levin Goldschmidt
Translated by John Koster

With an introduction by Willi Goetschel

BLOOMSBURY ACADEMIC
LONDON · NEW YORK · OXFORD · NEW DELHI · SYDNEY

BLOOMSBURY ACADEMIC
Bloomsbury Publishing Plc
50 Bedford Square, London, WC1B 3DP, UK
1385 Broadway, New York, NY 10018, USA
29 Earlsfort Terrace, Dublin 2, Ireland

BLOOMSBURY, BLOOMSBURY ACADEMIC and the Diana logo are
trademarks of Bloomsbury Publishing Plc

First published in 1976 in Switzerland as *Freiheit für den Widerspruch* by
Hermann Levin Goldschmidt © 1993 by Passagen Verlag, Ges.m.b.H., Vienna

First published in Great Britain 2020
This paperback edition published in 2021

English edition published by arrangement with Foundation Dialogik

Copyright © John Koster, 2020
Introduction © Willi Goetschel, 2020

John Koster has asserted his right under the Copyright, Designs and
Patents Act, 1988, to be identified as Translator of this work.

Cover design by Paul Smith
Cover image: "Red – C", 1981, 114.5 x 99.3 cm Courtesy of
The Gershon Iskowitz Foundation
Sean Weaver © Art Gallery of Ontario

All rights reserved. No part of this publication may be reproduced or transmitted
in any form or by any means, electronic or mechanical, including photocopying,
recording, or any information storage or retrieval system, without prior
permission in writing from the publishers.

Bloomsbury Publishing Plc does not have any control over, or responsibility for,
any third-party websites referred to or in this book. All internet addresses given
in this book were correct at the time of going to press. The author and publisher
regret any inconvenience caused if addresses have changed or sites have ceased
to exist, but can accept no responsibility for any such changes.

A catalogue record for this book is available from the British Library.

A catalog record for this book is available from the Library of Congress.

ISBN:	HB:	978-1-3500-7979-3
	PB:	978-1-3500-7978-6
	ePDF:	978-1-3500-7980-9
	eBook:	978-1-3500-7981-6

Typeset by Integra Software Services Pvt. Ltd.

To find out more about our authors and books visit www.bloomsbury.com
and sign up for our newsletters.

CONTENTS

Translating Goldschmidt: Philosophy and Rhetoric   viii

INTRODUCTION   1

Chapter 1
THE DISCOVERY OF CONTRADICTION   17
1   Contradiction from the beginning   17
2   Contradiction in thought   19
3   Contradiction in faith   20
4   Plato's dialectic   22

Chapter 2
FORGOTTEN AND OVERBLOWN CONTRADICTION   25
1   The unity of the Middle Ages   25
2   The All of the Middle Ages   26
3   The anxiety of the Middle Ages   28
4   The end of the Middle Ages   29

Chapter 3
REPRESSION OF CONTRADICTION   31
1   From opposition to contradiction   31
2   From Hegel to Marx and Kierkegaard   33
3   Mao Zedong's contradiction set free   36
4   The weakness of every dialectic   39

Chapter 4
ATTEMPTED DISPLACEMENT   41
1   Freedom of technology   41
2   Freedom through technology   42
3   Technology contra freedom   45
4   Freedom contra technology   48

Chapter 5
ATTEMPTED OPPRESSION   49
1   The completeness of the modern world   49
2   Totalitarian arrogation of totality   51
3   Fascist arrogation of force   53
4   The right to contradiction as the right to resistance   56

Chapter 6
ATTEMPTED ERADICATION ... 59
1. Attempted sabotage ... 59
2. Attempted postponement ... 62
3. Attempted dissipation ... 66
4. Attempted annihilation ... 68

Chapter 7
THE CHALLENGE OF CONTRADICTION ... 73
1. Outraged freedom ... 73
2. Freedom contra the state ... 75
3. Freedom through challenge ... 79
4. Freedom contra freedom ... 83

Chapter 8
THE CONTRADICTIONS OF FREEDOM ... 85
1. Freedom instead of subjugation ... 85
2. Freedom despite liberation ... 88
3. Freedom despite freedom ... 91
4. Limits of freedom—in freedom! ... 92

Chapter 9
THE UNAVOIDABLE CONTRADICTION ... 95
1. The old meaning ... 95
2. The lost meaning ... 97
3. The enduring meaning ... 99
4. The reclaimed meaning ... 104

Chapter 10
THE UNACCEPTABLE CONTRADICTION ... 107
1. Guilt and exculpation ... 107
2. Guilt and Turning ... 109
3. The good of Turning ... 112
4. In the end only good! ... 114

Chapter 11
CONTRADICTION SET FREE! ... 117
1. Dialogic instead of dialectics ... 117
2. Dialogic without dialogism ... 118
3. Set contradiction free! ... 121
4. Instead of sublation—*Aufgeräumtheit* ... 124

Chapter 12
IN CONTRADICTION TO THE WORLD   127
   1   The challenged environment   127
   2   Challenging maturity   130
   3   Costs claimed   133
   4   Required: Human beings!   137

Notes   140
Index   148
Index of Bible passages   151

Translating Goldschmidt: Philosophy and Rhetoric

Perhaps the most interesting challenge I faced as the translator of *Contradiction Set Free* concerns the distinction Goldschmidt maintains between philosophy and rhetoric. In the very first chapter, Goldschmidt treats of this distinction historically, suggesting that with the rise of sophism, rhetoric and philosophy parted ways for good:

> (T)he sophist's path leads to rhetoric, to "persuasion" [*Überredung*] and that means: ever further away from philosophy. The philosopher's path, however, leads to the dialectic of "conversation" [*Unterredung*], and that means: ever deeper into philosophy. (19)

This distinction between persuasion and conversation is fundamental to the critical impulse that sets Goldschmidt's conception of philosophy apart. Whereas rhetoric aims to literally "overspeak" its addressee, philosophy speaks "among" a diverse array of conflicting and contradictory truths. Yet this is not to say that philosophy can abstain from instrumental speech. After all, "the philosopher" is what Goldschmidt would call an ideal type. As a "real" philosopher, Goldschmidt of course had to avail himself of the persuasive tools that language offers.

Readers familiar with the Hegelian style may recognize that Goldschmidt's critique of the dialectic is aimed in part at its conception of language and human agency in regard to language: the way Hegelian puns and conceptual sleight of hand have long been used to reinforce a particular, Christian-inspired animism of the logos in which language itself is invested with agency and imagined as an overpowerful force.

Goldschmidt's wordplay has an entirely different character, and this difference extends his theoretical critique of the dialectic in a performative way on the level of style. In short, Goldschmidt's style, as an eminently inventive style, enacts his philosophical positions on human freedom, technology, and responsibility. We create language like we create any other technology, and at no point can we divest ourselves of responsibility for how we use it. Goldschmidt therefore has no use for inherent features of German that seem to reflect higher dialectical unity—Hegel's beloved "speculative concepts."

To be sure, Goldschmidt *plays* all the time with double and multiple meanings, to the point that some of his inventions—*Aufgeräumtheit*, for instance, a play on *Aufhebung*—must also be read as parodies of Hegelian concepts. And instead of using these features of language to overawe readers with glimpses of human subjectivity's symbolic straitjacket, he uses them to highlight, set free, and reinforce the real extent of human agency and responsibility.

The unique mixture of conceptual rigor and colloquial "straight talk" that characterizes this style reflects, on my view, Goldschmidt's full assumption of responsibility for language. We might say: his contradiction of Language. It is my hope that this translation conveys—or at least makes palpable—something of his singularly rebellious and philosophically mature style.

John Koster

INTRODUCTION

Willi Goetschel

Contradiction Set Free is above all a call to liberate us from the idea that there is something wrong where contradiction appears. As Goldschmidt notes early on in Chapter 1: "Where a contradiction makes itself heard, there, it is often thought, something is wrong—whereas the point is to grasp that it is there, where we encounter no contradiction, that something must be wrong."[1] For Goldschmidt, contradictions are not to be seen as roadblocks and obstacles to be set aside. They present potentially empowering opportunities for negotiating difference. Rather than deploring the challenge that contradictions present at every turn of our lives, Goldschmidt suggests we recognize the liberating power that a genuine acknowledgment of contradiction holds as promise. Release from its compulsive denial sets free the creative powers that the suppression of contradiction absorbed with its desire of neutralizing difference. Rather than resolution of contradiction by absorption into a monological scheme, Goldschmidt argues that the task we face consists in appreciating contradiction as a fundamental aspect of human experience. For Goldschmidt, contradiction is no longer reducible to an internalized failure of subjective insufficiency for which conventional logic used to make the individual responsible. Instead, contradiction emerges in Goldschmidt as gateway to a more open, inclusive, and comprehensive approach, a change of perspective that complicates but also expands and enriches the way we think, act, and experience life.

First published in 1976, *Contradiction Set Free* is the upshot of Goldschmidt's project of rethinking philosophy critically, i.e., dialogically, a project that goes back to the 1940s. Facing the catastrophic events of the Second World War and the Shoah, Goldschmidt and his contemporaries found themselves in a world that had profoundly changed with the indescribable loss of human lives that confronted modernity with the consequences of its own destructive forces. For those who survived the catastrophe, the question was how to recover the creative remnants of a Western culture that left its victims stranded at best if they were spared certain death. *Contradiction Set Free* presents Goldschmidt's answer: the monomaniacal fixation of monological thinking could only be overcome by turning to a dialogical approach that would no longer ignore or exclude contradiction but instead recognizes its emancipatory force.

During the same period of the 1940s in exile in the United States, Max Horkheimer, Theodor W. Adorno, Herbert Marcuse, and Eric Fromm responded to the catastrophe of the Shoah. To address its consequences radically and with critical resolve became part and parcel of the agenda of Critical Theory, while Martin Buber in Palestine and later the state of Israel resumed his work of further developing the "dialogical principle" he and Franz Rosenzweig had begun. Their movement took place at the same time while Emmanuel Levinas gave in Paris his own expression to the urgency of the dialogical imperative. In the context of these and other responses articulated by German Jewish émigré thinkers at the time, Goldschmidt's response from Zurich, launched from a similarly displaced situation, where he had fled from Berlin in 1938, assumes sharper contours.

If the 1960s gave rise to a new critical agenda with a radical vision for social and political justice, the recent commemorations of 1968 or the lack thereof remind us that the ideas of liberation envisioned at the time are yet to be realized. While they might seem to be dated they no less live on, to paraphrase Adorno, because the moment to realize them was missed.[2] Written during this period, Adorno's *Negative Dialectics* (1966), Paul Feyerabend's *Against Method: Outline of an Anarchistic Theory of Knowledge* (1975), and Goldschmidt's *Contradiction Set Free* (1976) have more in common than just temporal vicinity of the dates of their publication. They share a critical concern for rethinking the way we do philosophy, science, and envision life. The three books by Adorno, Feyerabend, and Goldschmidt demonstrate the undiminished topicality of their projects.

Goldschmidt's turn to dialogic powerfully resonates with Adorno's call for negative dialectics and Feyerabend's anarchistic theory of knowledge. They all embrace contradiction as doorway to opening up new approaches to truth and method rather than taking it as evidence of cognitive failure and a dead end for interaction.

A contemporary of Buber, Levinas, Feyerabend, Horkheimer, Adorno, Marcuse, Fromm, Habermas, and Derrida, Goldschmidt occupies a unique place between intellectual positions otherwise often considered incommensurate, adversarial, or mutually exclusive. Goldschmidt's stance however resonates upon closer examination more profoundly with his contemporaries when read in the larger context of the situation of this period. For these thinkers share a resolute opposition over and against the dominance of a philosophical praxis that was after all the very target of their critique. Lacking the benefit of academic affiliation and tenure, Goldschmidt enjoyed the kind of academic freedom academe rarely can offer. Unlike Levinas, however, with whom he shared the independent but demanding life of a free and unsalaried philosopher, Goldschmidt embraced his work in adult education as a unique opportunity to teach and interact with interlocutors whose independent minds became the testing ground for his ideas. For Goldschmidt, adult education offered the opportunity to share ideas in a congenial but critical, stimulating and at the same time discerning setting vital for genuine dialogue. For Goldschmidt, the task of rendering complex ideas accessible did not mean lowering the bar but a chance to explore them freely and unencumbered by the disciplinary protocol that dictates the institutional discourse of philosophy.

Goldschmidt saw himself as a free and independent writer, an unassuming but also emphatically charged term, which in German accentuates the act of writing as a critical form of assertion: *freier Schriftsteller*. An apparently innocuous designation, a *Schriftsteller* is a person who sets thought in writing (*Schrift*), i.e., puts the word forward as an intervention. In this regard, the designation of being a writer highlights the critical impulse of Goldschmidt's project as a process in which the act of writing sets contradiction free.

Born in Berlin in 1914 a few months before the beginning of the First World War, as he liked to point out, Goldschmidt immigrated to Switzerland in 1938 to escape persecution by the Nazis. At the University of Zurich, he studied philosophy. His dissertation *Nihilism in Light of a Critical Philosophy* (*Der Nihilismus im Licht einer kritischen Philosophie*, 1941)[3] understood Nietzsche's view of modernity as pervasively nihilistic less as a call for surrender than as a perceptive analysis of the cultural crisis that had led to Europe's darkest hour. For Goldschmidt, Nietzsche's gloomy diagnosis was a wake-up call that culture and philosophy had to change if their comatose state was to end. Amid the rubble of metaphysics that many saw as complicit with Europe's ruin, Goldschmidt saw Nietzsche as pointing a way out of the deadlock of a repressive culture that had begun to undercut the foundation of human existence it claimed to cultivate. At the zero hour of 1945 it had become clear that monological thinking and its unbridled claim to privileged access to knowledge were no longer a feasible option. It was no longer possible to close one's eyes to the havoc it had wrought. What was needed instead was, as Goldschmidt suggested, critical attention to Nietzsche's exhortation to modesty when it came to heed the epistemological limits of knowledge.

Following the breakthrough initiated by Hermann Cohen, Buber, and Rosenzweig, Goldschmidt embraced their turn to dialogical thinking but with a difference. Sharing crucial aspects of their thought, Goldschmidt moved past Cohen's neo-Kantian, Buber's phenomenological, and Rosenzweig's theological commitments. Casting dialogical thinking as a distinctly critical project, Goldschmidt dropped the ties to neo-Kantianism, the phenomenology of religion, and the theological agenda that marked the projects of Cohen, Buber, and Rosenzweig.

Like other German Jewish philosophers of his generation, Goldschmidt faced the same challenge that Cohen, Buber, Rosenzweig, Margarete Susman, Horkheimer, Adorno, Marcuse, and Hannah Arendt sought to address in their own ways. As Jews had eventually been accepted to the ranks of philosophers, their acceptance remained conditional on relinquishing their Jewish identity. Cohen had answered this challenge by upping the ante, arguing that it was precisely the sources of Jewish tradition that facilitated the universal and universally emancipatory outlook of philosophy. But this stand came at the costs of claiming the mantle of philosophy, whose disciplinary setup Buber, Rosenzweig, and Goldschmidt agreed needed first and foremost a rethinking from the bottom up. While Cohen had become the first Jewish philosopher to achieve the heights of a university chair of philosophy, he also would remain the only one to do so with the prominence, luster, and aura such a position carried during the Wilhelmine era.

While Jewish particularity was shunned as failing the German eligibility test, Cohen had turned the table on the exclusionary claims of universalism arguing that the universalism advanced in the notion of humanity relied on an inclusiveness anchored in the prophetic tradition's emancipatory embrace, heralded by the sources of Judaism. In the wake of this decisive turn, an individual's particularity was no longer to be considered a liability but, on the contrary, as their most empowering asset. Rather than a blind spot that needed to be blotted out, particularity provided the standpoint and perspective necessary to observe and reflect in the first place. For without such a position, there was no basis that grounded one's thinking. For Goldschmidt, recognition of one's particularity—its limits but also its singular scope—presents the condition for any philosophy aspiring to be critical. Illustrating this point with recourse to Heisenberg's uncertainty principle, he suggests that just as observation constitutes the nature of what is being observed, so every philosopher's standpoint enables but also delimits the epistemological process in constitutive fashion.

In the wake of the Shoah, Goldschmidt stood out as an early and distinct voice among Jewish philosophers. With the reception of Critical Theory's vision on the one hand selectively oblivious to its Jewish sources and dialogical thinking on the other assimilated into philosophy of religion as a subfield of philosophy, German Jewish identity was quickly broken up into seemingly opposite and contradictory constituents of its universal and particular aspects. Resisting the pressures of this dilemma German Jews faced in the postwar period, Goldschmidt sought to recover the ground in between these two positions where particularity would no longer be erased by exclusionary forms of universalism but recognized as the very condition of a genuinely open and inclusive approach with a universal impulse. Whereas Critical Theory seemed on the one hand to advocate the particular, it remained on the other ambivalent about openly embracing its own Jewish particularity to which it owed its most engaging impulse. In an opposite movement, the postwar reception of dialogical thinking focused on the religious dimension assimilating it to its particular theological demands, an appropriation that curiously neutralized the critical thrust of dialogical thinking.

While both Critical Theory and the exponents of dialogical thinking emphatically rejected the assimilation of Jewish identity to a binary scheme that cast Jews as minors ineligible for membership in majoritarian universalism as long as they would hold on to their particularity, Goldschmidt went a step further. True to the universal call to emancipation that so centrally informed both Critical Theory and dialogical thought that saw it paradigmatically exemplified in the biblical traditions and the shared commitment of both approaches to radically rethink philosophy in the light of this concern, Goldschmidt set out to address the question of philosophy from a non-exclusionary position that would no longer fix its lineage in exclusively constructed origins of Greek, German, or any other origin narrative. Resonating with the tradition of dialogical thinking and Critical Theory's desire for distinction from Hegelian dialectics, Goldschmidt's move to reimagine philosophy as dialogic took up a term initially introduced by Buber to which Goldschmidt however gave new critical meaning.

Whereas Cohen and Rosenzweig anchored their call for dialogical thinking in a return to the sources of Judaism, their counterpoint to the canon of Greek sources privileged by the discipline of philosophy, Buber couched his early dialogical writings in a theological shroud that channeled Jewish traditions in a less obvious, yet powerfully suggestive way. In response to the ultimate rejection with which their plea for inclusion had met, as they sought to assert Judaism's significance for a more inclusive vision of modernity, Goldschmidt raised the stakes by boldly knocking at philosophy's front door. With the demise of Europe's cultural hegemony after the Second World War, the Shoah, and the signs of a global shift, philosophy as it had lasted through the last years of Weimar Germany had come under scrutiny, its claims to supremacy becoming ever more problematic. Cohen, Buber, and Rosenzweig had been engaged in renegotiating the borders of philosophy at the margins. Goldschmidt went on to assert dialogical thinking as a distinctly philosophical necessity that could reimagine the project of philosophy in the wake of 1945. He did not argue for the primacy of one or another particular kind of philosophy but for rethinking how philosophy as a discourse of critical inquiry was to respond to the challenges posed by a modernity that experienced diversity, difference, and alterity as profoundly stirring issues that philosophers, whoever they were, could no longer ignore.

Contradiction Set Free takes us from philosophy's reluctant acknowledgment of contradiction as its originating condition to the recognition of such active difference as condition for critical philosophy. Departing from the standard narrative of the beginnings of philosophy in classic Greece, Goldschmidt widens the focus complementing it by interweaving another narrative that tracks Jewish tradition as it develops side by side with Greek thought. Attention to the constellation that the two traditions form sheds light on the cultural dynamics that made it possible for knowledge and religion to be considered to develop independently and in opposition to each other while obscuring the interface where the two traditions both connected to, and rejected, each other through a logic of (non-)contradiction that depends on the negation of the other on which its founding narratives are built. In Goldschmidt's examination of this muted interplay, a picture emerges of a rich and interconnected nexus of differences that help distinguish the complex forms of negotiations that allowed thought and faith to emerge as distinctly binary modes that rest on reciprocal denial.

Differently but profoundly resonating with these forms of renegotiating the terms of philosophy and its nexus with the narrative of its Greek origins, Horkheimer and Adorno's *Dialectic of Enlightenment* (1947) reexamined the *Odyssey* as a document reflecting the beginnings of self-destructive rationality whose epic dramatized the loneliness of the monological mindset whose rule is dictated by the repressive economy of domination by internalization of self-control, a counternarrative whose subversive thrust exposed the violence of the universal claims of the cultural primacy of the narrative of Greek philosophy with the spite of a revenge fantasy.

Apparently so different and at seemingly opposed ends, these and other German Jewish philosophers in exile faced the necessity to reimagine not only new forms of intellectual existence and affiliations but along with them the need to develop new forms of critical inquiry that would respond to the challenge of the situation they faced in the wake of the Second World War and the Shoah.

Philosophie als Dialogik (*Philosophy as Dialogic*) was Goldschmidt's early and direct response to this challenge. Initially the title of a lecture presented in the fall of 1944, *Philosophy as Dialogic* became the programmatic title of Goldschmidt's book of 1948.[4] With it Goldschmidt did not propose a new philosophy but a new approach to doing philosophy differently.

Whereas even a radical challenge of philosophy such as Rosenzweig's *The Star of Redemption* began with a discussion of cognition (*Erkennen*) as its opening bid, Goldschmidt was no longer willing to submit to philosophy's epistemological contract privileging thought's alleged primacy over action. Opening *Philosophy as Dialogic* in 1948 with a dialogue between thought and action, Goldschmidt countered the epistemological contract's erasure of the "and" that highlights the irreducibility of thought and action.[5] Exposing the partisanship of any claim to primacy on the part of either, the dialogue demonstrates how the contradiction of thought and action sets the stage for dialogical thinking to enter the fray. From the dialogue's conclusion, we glean that the dispute only deepens the irresolvable chasm between the two fiercely engaged opponents until they agree to at least one thing: to seek arbitration. The only arbitrator they are able to agree to is the philosopher, who, invited to declare a victor, replies that both parties are right albeit each within the limits of their respective perspectives. The dialogue ends with the following words:

> Is that still philosophy? thought and action reply at the same time. The philosopher responds: Why don't you care first about yourselves: whether you are still thought and action? But since you are asking: yes, philosophy—as dialogic ...[6]

Irreducible to each other, the incommensurability of thought and action requires an approach that recognizes the contradiction between them as the opposite of failure. Rather, Goldschmidt sees this contradiction as the starting point where philosophy arises beyond any wonder, bewilderment, or other form of reflective self-absorption as the founding narratives concerning the origin of philosophy suggest. Identifying instead the disjuncture between thought and action as the point of inception of philosophy as dialogic, Goldschmidt situates its trajectory at the interface in what he will call limit-case (*grenzsätzlich*) at the point of the contradiction that defines thought and action in mutually defining manner. Rudimentary and basic as it appears, this primeval scene situates philosophy from the beginning at the center of a contradiction whose pressures remain defining for the project of philosophy the way Goldschmidt gives it expression. As a result, philosophy itself is no longer conceived along the lines of privileging thought over action but in terms of the critical pressure that their contradiction produces. This way, Goldschmidt relocates philosophy outside the traditional framework of reflection and contemplation while refusing to simply invert the order by privileging action over thought. Rather, philosophy becomes the site where the contentions between the two are brought into the open as the dynamic tension that drives the project of philosophy. In other words, Goldschmidt comprehends the entry of philosophy directly to be right at the juncture of its constitutive contradiction between thought and action rather than the method of its riddance as conventionally conceived. This point is as it were inscribed at the opening ambit of Goldschmidt's approach and informs its critical trajectory.

For Goldschmidt, dialogic does not mean suspension of the principle of non-contradiction but merely the delimiting of the claim of a truth to the range of its validity. In the case of a contradiction between two mutually exclusive perspectives, each claim is true with regard to the specific context from which it arises and its truth is valid insofar as it does not reach beyond its own limits.[7] Like the change from Newton's classical physics to quantum physics, philosophy as dialogic does not render truth and knowledge as we have known them invalid but rather reconceives them as partial, context-dependent truths delimited by a contradiction where only the truth of one side can be claimed at a time. Just as quantum mechanics does not prove classical physics wrong but confines its range of application, Goldschmidt argues that dialogical thinking delimits the scope of every side of a contradiction to its field of vision. The way Heisenberg's uncertainty principle allows either for the perception of particles or waves but never of both at the same time, dialogic understands truth to be linked to the particular standpoint from which it arises. In both cases, the two sides of a contradiction present mutually exclusive vantage points to which their respective truths are confined.

In a similar way, thought and action contradict each other but form together the whole of human activity. While we are able to address only one at a time, each points to the other as its constitutive other. As the dialogue on thought and action suggests, rather than invalidating each other, thought and action in the face of their contradiction recognize each other in their own right as different yet interrelated aspects of a whole.

If the relationship between Critical Theory and dialogical thinking was strained to the degree of open conflict, the antagonism delineated for Goldschmidt a situation where the so different discourse of "particles" and "waves" suggested a contradiction that only highlighted the critical significance of the nexus between the two that its contradiction brought to the fore. Neither one nor the other would do the critical job on its own but recognition of their relationship as contradiction would allow for this tension to become critically productive.

Resonating with the critical concerns of both Critical Theory and dialogical thinking, Goldschmidt's approach charts a trajectory along the frontline that separates and interlinks the two respective agendas. Intersecting as they do like two sets that partly contradict and partly overlap, *Contradiction Set Free* charts the area of intersection where the most contested differences emerge. Stemming the double erasure to which the sidelining of the intersecting overlap amounts, Goldschmidt's push to set contradiction free opens the possibility of staking out the lines of agreement that need thus no longer to be obscured if not erased for the sake of theoretical assertion. For any such desire for cognitive privilege only undermines the critical thrust of their convergence.

For Goldschmidt like Rosenzweig, the "and" serves as a critical marker. Rather than merely additive and accumulative, it marks a difference whose distinctive feature creates the possibility of addressing alterity as a constitutive moment in the process of cognition. Connecting as it separates, distinguishing as it brings together, the "and" opens up at the same time as it interlinks. One is constitutive for the other, highlighting a two-directionality that serves as a reminder of the "and's" foundational meaning as correlative function that makes the process of cognition possible. The "and" is thus, epistemologically speaking, the condition of the possibility of knowledge. Critical thinking starts with an "and." Without it, as Rosenzweig had suggested, there is no relation in the first place.[8] Buber would reiterate this point with succinct clarity in his 1963 essay "Distance and Relation."[9]

For Goldschmidt, however, the theologically inflected mode of thinking that still informed Buber and Rosenzweig was no longer an option. While Cohen, Buber, and Rosenzweig saw the model for dialogical thinking prefigured in Judaism's most ancient, primarily biblical sources, Goldschmidt understood the dialogical model as a model to describe the culturally so productive yet at the same time profoundly conflicted dynamics of the experience of German Jewry. Whereas Cohen, Buber, and Rosenzweig had gestured towards a primary authenticity of Jewish tradition evidenced through its distinctly dialogical nature, Goldschmidt rendered the discourse of authenticity as unnecessary. Rather than mustering any sort of theological primacy to claim primeval intimacy with the divine, Goldschmidt's *The Legacy of German Jewry* (1957/2007) offered a case study in approaching cultural creativity in terms of a dynamic relationship of dialogical engagement.[10] Anticipating Derrida's later critique of Sartre's distinction between authenticity and inauthenticity, Goldschmidt's dialogical model of German Jewry demonstrated that for a tradition to be productive meant to embrace the "and" of its difference creatively—a move that exposes the desire for authenticity as marked by monological fixation.[11] Rather than arguing for the dialogical character of Jewish tradition, *The Legacy of German Jewry* argued for the critical significance of the dialogical model for understanding the cultural dynamics in modernity more generally.

If the 1960s was a time when it seemed that all we need is dialogue, the 1970s made it increasingly clear that such dreams were not to last. While dialogical thinking had become appropriated by ecumenical initiatives that seemed to reduce dialogue to an interfaith affair—a development that did not exactly bring the kind of attention to attract interest in philosophical quarters—politics suggested a similar move with dialogue enthusiastically adopted and domesticated to serve neutralizing tactics to facilitate co-option. As the cultural climate changed and the practice of streamlining dialogue to defuse difference became increasingly ingrained, Goldschmidt gave his approach a more pointedly critical edge. Returning a sharper bite to the emancipatory function of contradiction, which the dialectics of co-option had neutralized, Goldschmidt set contradiction free from the discursive regimes that had contained it by integration.

Such freedom for contradiction was directly linked to political freedom. As long as philosophy ignored this nexus, freedom itself was at risk. As Moses Mendelssohn had so succinctly remarked: "[T]he spirit of contradiction is not only a necessary consequence, but also often a wholesome underpinning of freedom and general well-being."[12] This decisive link between contradiction and freedom is key to dialogical thinking as Goldschmidt gives it more explicit articulation in *Contradiction Set Free*. As Cohen, Buber, and Rosenzweig defined freedom as the way we relate to one another dialogically, they critically engaged with the philosophical tradition that from Kant to Hegel had emerged as a discourse negotiating the foundational contradiction between the self's autonomy and the recognition by the other.

Whereas it is the "dialogical principle," as Buber called it,[13] that empowers us to be free as we become who we are through the encounter with the other, a dynamics of mutual exchange that represents the key condition for freedom as self-determination, Adorno and the Frankfurt School's emphasis on freedom's emancipatory thrust brought out the critical concern that informs Critical Theory's project to reclaim freedom from the hands of a liberal discourse that had sought to appropriate freedom for the purpose of a politics of containment. *Contradiction Set Free* spells out the implications of what in the 1970s seemed to have become a dead end for emancipatory hope. In the shadow of the overlap between dialogical thought and Critical Theory that overreaching forms of universalism had put under erasure freedom itself had become assimilated to a universal notion stripped from the particularities that are its necessary condition. Against this streamlining of freedom into a departicularized notion, *Contradiction Set Free* is a call to embrace the either-and-or of both the dialogical principle and the emancipatory concept of freedom consonant with the project of Critical Theory without having to compromise any of their respective strengths. Rather, as a result of the embrace of a decisive "and" Goldschmidt argues to address contradiction's fundamental significance for freedom openly and head on.

But not all opposition amounts to a contradiction. Distinguishing between opposition and contradiction, Goldschmidt points out a crucial difference:

> Opposition and contradiction are two different things. Opposition is the Either-Or of the "alternative," or alternation; contradiction is the Either-And-Or of conflict: a collision.[14]

While opposites (*Gegenteile*) of an opposition (*Gegensatz*) exclude but also complement each other together adding up to the whole of its unity, contradiction presents something "dually whole" as mutually contradictory: a collision. The Either-Or indicates opposite possibilities where each in its own way presupposes the opposite it excludes.

> Contradiction, on the other hand, involves insertion into the tension of an Either-And-Or, in which the two possible decisions cannot be unified. It is therefore also never enough to have made a decision. Rather than alternating

with the other decision, in contradiction one decision collides with the other, and each calls, with the equal weight of an entire reality, its coexistent and co-present [*mitgegenwärtig*] other irreconcilably into question.[15]

The "Either-And-Other" of this contradiction calls for an altogether different logic. Expressing a confrontation that takes place between two sides of a contradiction, conflict and tension between two mutually exclusive claims make it impossible to simply choose one opposite over the other as the opposites of an opposition would allow. Rather, the "Either-And-Or" signals the irreducibility of a clash to a final resolution. Instead, contradiction as Goldschmidt understands it requires a logic that does justice to both sides recognizing each side's genuine legitimacy while conceding so within each standpoint's respective limits that define them. The approach of recognizing each side's legitimacy while acknowledging the limits where the other's equally legitimate contrary claim arises without imposing any kind of criteria external to this contradiction to resolve it from a "third" point of view but instead to negotiate it from a contradiction immanent position of creative engagement between the parties: this is what Goldschmidt calls dialogic.

Dialogue and dialogism

"Set contradiction free!" is a call for recognition of contradiction that goes beyond the acknowledgment by dialectic:

> [D]ialogic remains open even to dialectics, which it contradicts and which contradicts it, whereas dialectics goes off on yet another imperious rampage every time it encounters the contradiction of dialogic.[16]

But does not this greater openness dilute into an any-thing-goes-dialogism that becomes hypertolerant and all-permissive to the degree of complete self-destruction? Dialogic, Goldschmidt insists, is not a call for dialogism. Distinguishing four kinds of dialogism, he rejects all four of them as travesties that hijack dialogue to neutralize the effects of contradiction by pluralization into a zero sum game. The four dialogisms are: (1) overestimation of the diversity of contradiction as if because of it neither more unambiguity nor decisiveness were possible, (2) surrender to the other as if only the other would be authorized to determine the outcome of a dialogue with only one speaker, (3) pandialogism, i.e., the desire to dialogue with everybody and all at the same time, and (4) the literally irresponsible pluralogics to expose oneself simultaneously to any number of contradictions instead of committing to answer one at a time as it calls one to account.

To set contradiction free is thus a project that is decisively different from promoting convergence, coexistence, coordination, cooperation, complementarity, and tolerance, which ultimately remain merely variants of monological thinking incapable of genuine appreciation of the critical significance of the other and its contradiction. Whereas dialogism is the effort to dissolve tension and conflict, it incapacitates the genuine engagement with contradiction and thus forestalls the possibility to avail itself of contradiction's emancipatory thrust that critical attention to contradiction holds in store. Dialogism, in other words, turns contradiction into a dialogue in name only reducing it to the baseline minimum of a conversation of two as if such a formalist approach would already present the answer to the conflict it ultimately dissolves into chatter. Dialogism domesticates contradiction by affirmatively acknowledging it while at the same time containing it.

Anarchism

The critical significance of taking contradiction seriously, however, is not yet fully understood as long as its dynamics are not more completely explored as the brief but succinct examination of anarchism demonstrates. The heart of the book, Chapter 7, highlights anarchism's paradigmatic significance for understanding freedom's dynamic character. Committed to reclaim individual freedom against any form of domination and control by the state, society, or other corporate or collective power, anarchism is the stubborn reminder of the contradictory nature of freedom. Posing the question of freedom in radically provocative manner, anarchism exposes the structural grip of institutional pressure to which individual agency is subjected in modernity. While in contrast to William Godwin, Pierre-Joseph Proudhon, and Max Stirner, Mikhail Bakunin had embraced "direct action" and the use of violence, Goldschmidt reminds us, it was Leo Tolstoy who at the same historical moment would champion nonviolence as the hallmark of a more sustainable commitment to anarchism:

> In trying to oppose violence to violence, you, working men, do what a man bound with ropes would do if, to free himself, he should tug at the ropes: he would only tighten the knots which fetter him. The same is true as regards your attempts by means of violence to take away what is withheld from you by means of violence.[17]

It was Proudhon who early on made it clear that freedom stood at the center of this concern:

> Freedom! This is the first and last word of every social philosophy.[18]

But what then is freedom? Tracking the anarchist debates about power and violence, Goldschmidt understands the dissent among anarchists as testimony to the contradictory nature of freedom itself. Ultimately freedom, as the anarchist dissent and their disagreement among each other demonstrate, resists clear and simple conceptualization because rather than a state or static condition, freedom is the expression of a process of negotiating between different exigencies in context-dependent situations. Freedom's contradictory nature, the anarchist discourse highlights however, is not a sign of an insufficiency or flaw but evidence of freedom's dynamic to bring out contradiction's emancipatory force. Rather than the fixed identity of a given, freedom arises through the process of individuation that refuses imposition of any external norms as it develops its sense of self autonomously in a process in which autonomy emerges as the effect of a continuous process of negotiation.

At the interface between institutional, societal, and individual forms of power, anarchism spells out the dynamic and contradictory character of freedom whose nature remains elusive and resistant to conceptualization because it assumes concrete contours only where it is actualized in the moment of a particular instantiation. Stubbornly resisting appropriation and domestication, anarchism remains resiliently true to the contradiction's critical impulse.

This is true for classic anarchism as it was expressed in Bakunin, Peter Kropotkin, Stirner, Gustav Landauer as well as for the Paris Commune and the Spanish anarchists. If the demise of Spanish anarchism in 1937 was considered the end of anarchism, Goldschmidt notes that the 1960s witnessed its return with the student protests in Berlin and at Berkeley albeit in the name of a Marxism that obscured its anarchist roots. With the return of these protests and the sparking of student revolts, Marcuse rose to the front spearheading the fourth epoch of anarchism, an epoch, Goldschmidt notes, whose end is not yet in sight. For Marcuse's "great refusal" has continued to spawn new forms of contradiction for the sake of a freedom that continues to be under precarious siege and often where its rhetoric runs highest.

Giving voice to the primacy of freedom above everything else, anarchism ultimately runs into contradictions of its own. But, as Goldschmidt reminds us, this is not anarchism's fault but the logical consequence of freedom's own contradictory nature. Anarchism's insight into the central significance of freedom however remains so vital because its loss is not just a surrender to the powers that be—of the political, social, cultural, and intellectual order—but because with its surrender thought and action are reduced to mere instruments of a scenario where human agency has no longer meaning. Today's plethora of dystopian anxieties and the search for ever-new forms of refusal are a sign of how deeply this issue has come to affect the current condition. But to condemn anarchism as violent is a mythologization that blames the protester for what they protest, a mythologization that shifts the responsibility of the use of violence only one more time to the victims of the violence against which they stand up.

Goldschmidt concludes: "It is not only freedom that is needed, but contradiction set free."[19] For freedom alone is not enough. In addition contradiction needs to be set free and more exactly the other's contradiction:

> Everyone and everything else must also have its say, not only each person him- or herself.[20]

The contradictions of freedom as freedom's internal challenge are the subject of Chapter 8. The contradictions that freedom faces from within are the results of the process of liberation and emancipation, which, at every stage, redefines freedom anew. As a result, from antiquity to the present freedom emerges as a dynamically evolving process with no end in sight because every assumption of a teleological scheme with a final end point would undermine the very notion of freedom itself. The contradiction between freedom and determination, freedom and law is thus constitutive for freedom. Goethe's classic formulation that it is law that sets us free is for Goldschmidt less a paradox than a reflection of the irresolvable dynamics that defines freedom's Promethean nature. While Hegel's dialectics recognized the entangled interplay between the push and pull of what has come to be called the master-slave dialectics, the Hegelian schematism projected the contradictory character of freedom on a temporal scheme that anticipates a teleological structure with an end however delayed or distant that endpoint. Supplementing Hegel's dialectic with a dialogical addendum, Goldschmidt casts off the harness that locked freedom into a scheme of a narrative of historical progression. Instead, Goldschmidt recognizes freedom's own contradictoriness as empowering momentum of freedom's emancipatory thrust.

Irreducible to arbitrariness, willfulness, freedom of choice, and other forms of voluntarist notions of freedom, Goldschmidt addresses freedom as a continuous process of self-determination through which the self emerges as an ever-evolving agency defined by its interrelationships, i.e., a process of dialogical negotiation. Setting "limits out of freedom—in freedom"—as the heading of the concluding section of Chapter 8 puts it—highlights the dialogical character of freedom as the expression of a relational effect defined by the ever different relationships of its respective constituents that no longer allows for abstraction from its particularities. As Goldschmidt wonders in the chapter's concluding section: "Why shouldn't that which freedom proclaims to others—the diversity of contradictions—also apply to freedom itself?!"[21]

Right to resistance and contradiction

If in an anachronistic move fascism's arrogation and totalitarianism's presumption of force seek to eradicate contradiction at the moment its denial and erasure have become self-destructive, Chapter 5 argues that Adorno's call for "an education to contradiction and resistance" is not enough. Rather, Goldschmidt argues for the recognition of the right to contradiction as the underlying and decisive necessity to enable resistance and maturity (Mündigkeit). For, resistance and eventual maturity are impossible without a resolute acknowledgment of the foundational role of contradiction for freedom.[22]

But these are not the only dangers that modernity holds in store, Chapter 6 points out. Sabotage by manipulation—what Marcuse called "secret temptation"[23]—is another way to mute contradiction just as futurology presents yet another equally seductive fantasy. But anticipation of the future with the promise of resolution of each and every challenge mortgages the present against a future forever delayed, which, in fact, has already begun. A third form of eradication is dissipation by blinkered expertocracy. However, reducing contradiction to a sign of error rather than to comprehend its significance by exposing a truth of its own is to forsake the promise of liberation that attention to conflict and collision hold out where contradiction is no longer repressed but given the chance to come to the fore.

There is yet, Chapter 9 shows, another kind of contradiction we encounter that cannot be negated because they present the condition of life itself: life and death, health and illness. The desire for reduction of contradiction to a noncontradictory existence would be inhuman and deprive us of the meaning of life. There is no possibility for simple alternatives of an Either-Or. Instead they present us with a world of Either-And-Or that requires a different approach that no longer seeks to avoid the unavoidable but confronts it in productive manner. Rather than excluding and removing death and illness from society, Goldschmidt suggests that contradiction set free empowers those suffering from illness and those being wounded to become equal fellow human beings, each in their own way enriching the world of those who only know the world from the vantage point of what they imagine is "normal" life and health.

Technology and nature's contradiction

Just as freedom resists unilateral definition but emerges as the result of creative negotiation, technology can both enable and disable freedom, merely amplifying both the possibility to gain more freedom thanks to technology or to become ever-more subject to the powers of technology as technology increases our own power but with it also its hold on us. For Goldschmidt, the answer of whether technology liberates or enslaves us is a question of how we relate to technology, Chapter 4 shows. Here, too, setting this particular case of contradiction free liberates us from subjection to a power that is only as strong as we allow it to become. But rather than a dialectic development of necessity from which there is no escape as technology-blind reasoning might have it, technology's impact on freedom is merely a function of how we relate to the challenge that technology poses.

Beyond the limits humanity has been able to overcome and will overcome there also remain limits that cannot be broken through: "nature contradicts" as well.[24] While Goldschmidt's 1970s call for the acknowledgment of nature and planet earth as partners rather than humankind's property that might be used as humanity sees fit might have been ahead of its time, the sense of urgency concerning the challenges we face in the age of the Anthropocene have now caught up with us. So, too, has the notion that an economy that downplays the problem of the social costs of private industry is no longer feasible.

For taking responsibility for the costs of productivity is not just a function of economic prudence and ethical necessity but has become a matter of sheer existential survival. Dodging responsibility will eventually lead to an irreversible dead end as the opening sentence of the book's concluding section points out:

It is not to other humanities of other stars, which are mere excuses—just like the stores of resources supposedly waiting on other planets to replace the earth's depleted resources are mere excuses—that humanity addresses its "Thou," but to the environment with which it has collided and will continue to collide in increasingly contradictory ways in the future.[25]

Besides openness to the world (*Weltoffenheit*) there is therefore an additional step required: to grasp the meaning of being called into question by the world and the contradiction through which the world confronts humanity with its responsibility in the case of each and every human being. Facing its final challenge, humanity can no longer escape the call for maturity because its bare existence has now become dependent on whether or not humanity lives up to its challenge:

It is the environment that presents humanity—at the height of "dialogic without dialogisms"—with responsibilities of which humanity on its own may not have been aware, and which it may at first hardly understand and possibly be reluctant to hear, yet which it must, though even more reluctantly, nonetheless accept.[26]

Maturity, Goldschmidt reminds us, ultimately rests on the recognition of the other as the necessary condition of each and every individual's opportunity to achieve maturity whether the other is our neighbor or whoever we face in immediate encounter over and against us, or whether it is the environment, i.e., nature which confronts us as another that contradicts. Given the dialogical dynamics that underlies the construction of individuality, Goldschmidt's call for maturity is neither a call for individual growth alone nor simply a shifting of responsibility to society at large, i.e., everybody and nobody in particular. Rather, humanity's maturity hinges on the condition that every individual human being be given the opportunity to achieve maturity since humanity consists in nothing else than the sum total of each and every of its individuals. "Meaning and fruitfulness and joy, freedom and peace, are," as Goldschmidt notes, "either secured for all, or certain for none."[27] The survival and continuation of humanity, Goldschmidt concludes, ultimately depends on humanity's maturity, i.e., the maturity of all humans beings together.

A book of the 1970s, *Contradiction Set Free* is no less a book for our times. It continues to speak with undiminished topicality to today's issues and especially those that confront us with increasing urgency. If anything has changed it is the call to recognize that the need for free critical thinking and the right to contradiction has become the more urgent the more we witness worldwide the consequences of repressing the contradictions on which modernity rests. The sense of humanity's trajectory on "spaceship earth" where space and resources are finite has not been lost on the current debates although prospects that we act on it appear to be as dim as ever. On the other hand there appears to be a compensatory relish to entertain dystopian fantasies. It seems that in either case outward projection of the contradictions we face but fail to confront naturalizes them as if they were merely glitches or errors in the production process of knowledge and as if erasing difference in compliance with the law of non-contradiction would yield the relief that it renders impossible. In contrast, *Contradiction Set Free* argues for a critical openness and invites us to welcome difference and alterity as harbingers of hope and emancipation.

Chapter 1

THE DISCOVERY OF CONTRADICTION

Contradiction from the beginning

Every human being is a whole person or can at least become one. This means the human being is confronted with the universe as something that is, like itself, both singular and whole. If this at once alarmingly weak, and on its own for the most part helpless human creature begins to doubt that it is—all on its own—nonetheless a whole human being (or at least capable of becoming one), it finds itself supported by the singularity and wholeness of the universe, which guarantees by its existence the human being's as well. Furthermore, the human being is connected to the other humans, each of which is nonetheless, like itself, a whole person all on its own. No matter how intimate their connections with each other or their oneness with the universe may be, humans are, however, never repetitions of each other. The human other, each singular and whole in its own right, is never the same, but always a different person. Humans don't repeat each other; they contradict each other.

The contradictions that arise between people, in faith and in thought, and between faith and thought, are, from the very beginning, just as fundamental as the individual and collective encounter with the unity of the All. Faced with such contradictoriness, is not this unity merely unified [*vereinheitlicht*] diversity, that is to say, ultimately only an imagined unity? And is not diversity then here the ultimate: a diversity that, while it can be united [*vereinigen*], cannot be, cannot ever be, unified? Yet the predominating tendency prefers unity and is full of mistrust in the face of diversity.

It is supposed that the noncontradictory, uniform whole has an advantage over the whole of contradictory diversity, even though the whole accessed through diversity is equally complete and far more emancipatory. Where a contradiction makes itself heard, there, it is often thought, something is wrong—whereas the point is to grasp that it is there, where we encounter no contradiction, that something must be wrong. For unification, which always boils down to enforced conformity [*Gleichschaltung*], does not safeguard freedom; contradiction does: by virtue of ruling out every unification. Yet deeply engrained prejudices block contradiction's path to freedom, even though its liberation, and its liberation alone, can lead to freedom's consummation.

For that singularity and wholeness as which every human being must realize itself also compels it beyond itself towards a unity that embraces the entire universe. This is one of the motives behind the seductive preference for unity in regard to humanity and the universe. The other motive is the no less sublime experience (which makes and leaves an overpowering impression) that, although spirit is perceived by the individual—and by the individual alone—the truth it makes accessible to the individual is nonetheless supra-individual.

That the breakthrough of spirit and to spirit also marks the truth of individuality as its right to contradiction, and that spirit itself represents, from the very beginning, a contradictory breakthrough, has always attracted less attention than the breakthrough to the law, this perception of the universal. The mutually contradictory individuals who grasp the spirit in words, and the contradictory particulars with which they substantiate it, seem less essential than the universality of the spirit that is verified through and because of them.

Nonetheless, in addition to truth's universality, its contradictoriness has always accompanied it as well, posing a twofold contradiction from the very beginning. This contradiction confronts the truth as a different truth and—within every truth—it confronts the perception of this truth as a different perception of the same truth. In this way, the contradiction that confronts the truth from the outside is founded in the historical event of the simultaneity of two breakthroughs to spirit. Owing to them, this one and only spirit is henceforth faith as well as knowledge: truth by virtue of revelation and truth by virtue of reason.

Yet although this contradictoriness of spirit is from the very beginning, as the opposition of faith and knowledge, an equally important feature of the breakthrough to spirit, it has gone ignored for centuries. The religious awe [*Ergriffenheit*] of biblical Judaism and the conceptual illumination of ancient Greek philosophy proceeded alongside one another, with revelation beyond reason holding sway on the one side and reason beyond revelation holding sway on the other. The truth of faith prevailed without being challenged by the literally far-fetched truth of reason. And the truth of reason prevailed without any sense of the contradiction posed to it by revelation, because it had only the religiosity of its own Greek populace as a reference point, a piety that was no match for philosophy.

Ever since, after Plato's death, Aristotle left Athens and encountered a Jew for the first time in Assos in Asia Minor, "who in the intimate converse he maintained with many cultivated persons imparted more than he received,"[1] and since the time of his pupil Alexander the Great Greeks and Jews had unavoidably encountered each other without being able to meld. They never had to face the mutual contradiction between faith and knowledge, which they, together, had brought to expression. This predicament would instead determine the fate of the Middle Ages. Yet neither the creators of revealed religion nor the creators of philosophy, who were each able to avoid the mutual contradiction they had ushered into the world, had escaped contradiction as such. They were not spared that contradiction which, within every truth, encounters the perception of this truth as a different perception of the same truth.

1. The Discovery of Contradiction

Contradiction in thought

Philosophy begins because, in addition to a wealth of knowledge that helps us better master the world and life, there also exists, between the laws of the universe and the reason that reflects them, a perfect consonance called truth. The human being is not just anyone who also knows something, but rather the one whose knowledge perceives the law according to which it itself and the world in its entirety bring about their effects, in spite of the weakness, misery, helplessness, and brevity of every individual human life. Differently, however, than in the sciences, which now also began to develop and for which philosophy also vouches, the truth that is philosophy's concern never ceases to be called into question. To want to merely complete it is not enough.

That the truth exists and that humans perceive it does not foreclose the possibility of perceiving the truth in the guise of a formal universality from which the particulars dissipate, or as a plethora of characteristics that simply cannot be unified on account of the particulars. Nor does it preclude perceiving the truth as spirit rather than as substance, or as being (if becoming is not presupposed) or even the reverse: as substance instead of spirit, becoming instead of being! Nothing flows, as judged from the being of spirit, and everything flows when one attends to substance and its becoming: both are true.

Philosophy hardly existed before it appeared in the plural, without therefore ceasing to be philosophy in the singular: truth as such. Parmenides and Heraclitus, who during the same decades of the closing sixth and beginning fifth centuries already confronted one another spatially as the west of Lower Italy and the east of Asia Minor, challenged the breakthrough of spirit to philosophy, which had been ushered in by Thales, with the fact of this first fundamental contradiction. They thereby challenged philosophy to take up that search for truth that constitutes its unique mandate. That there is truth, and that human beings perceive it, is not thrown into question by the fact that the perceptions of this truth contradict one another. Neither sophism nor philosophy, whose journeys had just begun and whose paths would soon part for good, is daunted by the contradictoriness of perceiving truth. But the sophist's path leads to rhetoric, to "persuasion" [*Überredung*] and that means: ever further away from philosophy. The philosopher's path, however, leads to the dialectic of "discussion" [*Unterredung*], and that means: ever deeper into philosophy.

Both the sophist, who lives from the truth, and the philosopher, who lives for it, brought an end to pre-Socratic philosophy. This pre-Socratic philosophy had, in its attempt to press forward to a truth without contradiction, thereby made manifest the contradiction of the perceptions of this truth. For the sophist and the philosopher alike, contradiction is from now on the point of departure—whereby with reference to Plato, and in the formulation of Max Weber, sophism and philosophy are understood to be ideal types. We can thus leave aside the question that arises vis-à-vis its real type, of whether this or that sophist wasn't also a philosopher, and whether many a philosopher wasn't also a sophist; Socrates, for instance, maybe even Plato?

The sophist—sophist in the sense of the ideal type—uses the contradictoriness of truth in order to end up being right no matter what, whereas the philosopher—philosopher in the sense of the ideal type—takes the truth for the sake of its contradictoriness upon him- or herself as a goal which, against everything that seems to already be in the right, always still remains to be fought for. Because the truth is *contradictorily* true, the sophist is prepared, with the best conscience in the world and for a lucrative payoff, to stand up for whichever side employs him or her at any particular moment. The philosopher on the other hand is prepared—because the contradictory truth is *true*—to stand up for it without demanding any pay. May the philosopher's "philo-sophia," which for love of truth builds on truth's claim and its claim alone, never fully satisfy either side! The philosopher would rather risk his or her life than risk merely achieving success in it.

Contradiction in faith

The same separation that, in view of the contradictoriness of the concept, leads in one direction to philosophy and in the other to sophism also creates a division within revealed religion, owing to the contradictions of its awe: the distinction between true and false prophecy. The true messenger's concern is the truth, with success being neither here nor there, whereas for the false messenger, the back-and-forth of truth is a means to success.

Still, the contradiction between the truth of religion and that of philosophy went unremarked. But there was also—like the contradiction within philosophizing—already contradiction within religiosity and with it the pressure to choose between the "sophistic" approach of the false prophet and the "philosophical" approach of the true prophet. Instead of the perfect consonance between the laws of the universe and the reason that pursues them in contemplation as conceived on the Greek side of antiquity, Jewry conceives of the human creature's perfect consonance with the purposes of creation. On the other side of the awakening to the concept, this awakening to awe, which offered certainty rather than knowledge and was thus faith, is also exposed to contradiction. Here as everywhere, its challenge recalls at the very least that in every truth, the perception of this truth encounters other perceptions of the same truth.

It was, to be sure, the human being as such which, as the sole being and only as a whole human being, entered into certainty, so that to it—who is not the creator of the universe, but merely one of its creatures—the purposes of creation from its beginning to its end would be revealed, and so that it, this human in the singular, would able to follow their guidance. But the same thing was also revealed which the Greeks had realized when their individual spirit conceived of itself as the likeness of the supra-individual spirit, capable of thinking the law of its self and that of the universe from their first cause to their final implication: the contradictoriness of the perceptions of the truth! In light of the truth of faith, the biblical human, created in the image of its creator, catches sight of itself in the contradictoriness of the perceptions of man and woman or victim and murderer, and of the multiplicity of languages, despite the one original language of all humans.

"God created man in His image, in the image of God He created him," it reads without qualification, and in the same sentence continues "male and female He created them" (Gen. 1:27). Or, putting it more radically into contradiction, without for that reason calling into question the wholeness of every individual human being, its individuality in its complete responsibility for itself and creation: "It is not good for man to be alone; I will make a fitting helper, a counterpart [*Gegenüber*] for him" (2:18, trans. mod.). For animals, these living beings subject to human language, prove to be an insufficient companion for human life. While giving them their names, which are chosen by humans, "no helper suitable to be his counterpart" [*keine Hilfe, ihm Gegenpart*] (2:20, trans. mod.) is to be found, as Martin Buber's translation of 2:18 and 2:20 puts it. In addressing animals, only the human monologue unfurled and continues to unfurl, without enabling that enrichment which can only be opened up by dialogue, which humans need in order to be the whole human beings they really are.

It is only when the man is given bone of his bone and flesh of his flesh that he calls out joyfully, "This one at last!" (2:23, trans. mod.). Repeated in this way by another human, the human who is now enabled to carry on a dialogue finds himself facing a human who is different from himself. The other who shares his language with him is capable of contradicting him.

To the same end, the Bible then immediately presents another state of paradise, this time one in which two men's unclouded brotherhood erupts "in the course of time" (4:3) with the internal contradictoriness of this and every human siblinghood. According to biblical linguistic usage, this is the first time that "sin couches at the door" and that the human is obliged to master it (4:7). Real human life begins with committing the misdeed, its "unacceptable contradiction"; the subjugation of evil, which is as possible as it is necessary, is not thereby weakened so much as crystallized. The evil of the evil person, which is evil always and under all conditions as the good that is "owed," opens, by virtue of this owing [*Schuld*], the possibility of Turning [*teshuva*] from guilt. When Cain asks: "Am I my brother's keeper?" (4:9), the acceptance of the contradiction he rejects crystallizes into a mandate and a necessity.

The "Tower of Babel" (11:1–9) makes the same point. As in the case of the contradictions that arise between Adam and Eve and Abel and Cain, this story also tries to show, on the basis of the acceptance of a debt, that its consequence—the diversity of human languages—is not a contradictoriness to be overcome, but rather one to be sustained; and that without it, the history that does exist—a historical reality meaningful and creative in equal measure—would not. The different languages of the different peoples, which only the ever-meddling prejudice against contradiction laments as "confusion," are the flipside of the fact that humans have the power of language and are capable of reaching agreements. The upshot of the contradiction between each language, which excludes all unification, has to be acknowledgment of that original oneness. But insisting upon that oneness does not bring the languages together but has instead brought about a separation by virtue of which they may finally be brought together for real.

Like the paradise lost by Adam and Eve or Abel and Cain, the loss of the peoples' paradise that existed before the building of Tower of Babel does not cancel the wholeness of humanity that Abraham can only now set forth to gather together (12:1 et seq.). Now and only now can the once cursed earth (3:17) again be included in the blessing of the gathering now commencing upon it. This earth is the very ground and foundation of world history and of the story, which was only just beginning, of the salvation of all peoples and of humankind: "All the families of the earth shall be blessed!" (12:3, trans. mod.).

Plato's dialectic

But it is philosophy that conceptualizes what biblical awe can only narrate. The contradictoriness of the perceptions of truth, which pre-Socratic philosophy had brought to light, becomes in Plato's hands a "method," that is to say a "guide" to the path towards truth. It is contradictoriness itself and as such that will henceforth lead to truth, although—owing to this contradictoriness—one can never proceed from truth. The differing, unavoidably differing claims to truth offer points of departure whose contradictory back-and-forth (called "dialectic" in Greek) can, according to Plato's teaching, be used by philosophers (although it was merely exploited by the sophists to insist on the correctness of their own or their clients' positions) to lead towards truth.

Despite the contradictions among their perceptions, truth never stops being true or being the same, sole truth for all human beings. Like the sophist, Socrates boasts of his knowledge, but as the philosopher, who with this insight overcomes sophism, he boasts of knowing that he knows nothing and that he is thus the wisest of all people![2] With this triadic move—which stopped neither at the truth of no knowledge nor at that of not-knowing, and with this first, noteworthy example of how to proceed from the positing, or thesis, of knowledge, by way of the counter-positing, or antithesis, of not-knowing, to the continuation, or synthesis, of wisdom—the guide or method of the dialectic was already complete, even though its long journey of exposing truth by taking contradictions into account had only just begun.

This amounted to a "turning around of the soul" [*psyches periagoge*],[3] as Plato himself understood and elaborated it: a confidence-inspiring turning around of the soul of truly enduring significance, even if this first dialectic (or first-stage dialectic) lacked the dimension of history. Hegel would integrate it into the dialectic only after history—and the dialectic of history—had been brought to expression by biblical Judaism. As the first to succeed in thinking this accomplishment all the way through, Hegel thereby became the creator of the second-stage dialectic. Faith itself submitted its contribution to the dialectic in the form of an embodied testimony, without also raising its awe to the level of the concept.

The severe announcement of Isaiah, for example: "Hear, indeed, but do not understand; see, indeed, but do not grasp [...] Till the towns lie waste without inhabitants and houses without people, and the ground lies waste and desolate" (6:9–11), whereby he maintains his certainty that justice and teaching will flourish between the peoples and that they will stop training for war (2:4), demonstrates a conception of history—which Plato had left aside—that is just as dialectical as Plato's world of spiritual development. The same is true of the realization that descends upon Jeremiah, and ultimately seems thoroughly sensible to him, that there are also false prophets who can, on account of the contradictions inherent in the perception of the truth, codetermine the course of history and succeed over long periods of time, whereas the true prophets build on a future verification, even though staying faithful to it is more likely to cost them their life than to bring them success (27:12 et seq.; 28:1 et seq.; 38:1 et seq.).

"Many a road," as it is then put in Proverbs, "may seem right to a man, but in the end it is a road to death" (14:12; 16:25). And "Do not believe!" writes John, already anticipating in essence all the philosophical struggles that have ensued since Hegel and Marx over the distinction between authentic and false consciousness: "Do not believe every spirit, but test the spirits to see whether they are from God; for many false prophets have gone out into the world" (1 John 4:1).

But the accomplishment of philosophy, Plato's path-breaking achievement, which is still worth thinking through, was to have conceived of this back-and-forth of the spirit's truth-claims not as fallacy, but as the objectively necessary and sensible method for proceeding towards truth. Instead of resting content, in the wake of the awe of faith, with that testimony of truth which will only emerge in its ultimately triumphant completeness later—when God is all in all (1 Cor. 15:28)—to retroactively verify its witnesses; and instead of sophistically standing still between the mutually contradictory truth-claims of the here and now in order to win the day now for one, now for the other side, the philosopher connects all the claims to truth to the dialectic of the triad's ongoing, progressive approach to it.

Only the dialectical method, Socrates says in Plato's *Republic*, does not stop at a single assumption of truth, but instead returns to the point of its departure in order to win a stable footing. In so doing it draws "the eye of the soul, which is really buried in a kind of barbaric mire, and leads it upwards," using all the relevant arts and sciences as handmaids and helpers in the work of turning the soul around.[4] Something unique and new, comparable to the Promethean conquest of fire, by which humankind dared to strike out on its own, has been introduced here, as Plato has Socrates jubilantly announce:

> A gift of gods to men, as I believe, was tossed down from some divine source through the agency of a Prometheus together with a gleaming fire; and the ancients, who were better than we and lived nearer the gods, handed down the tradition that all the things which are ever said to exist are sprung from one and many and have inherent in them the finite and the infinite. [...] [B]ut the wise men of the present day make the one and the many too quickly or too slowly, in haphazard fashion, and they put infinity immediately after unity; they disregard all that lies between them, and this it is which distinguishes between the dialectic and the disputatious methods of discussion.[5]

Although it considers every claim to truth as well as what lies midway between them, and investigates the different points of view and their shared whole neither too quickly nor too slowly and without exploiting the contradictions that become visible along the way only in order to prove itself solely in the right, nonetheless this first-stage dialectic—like the second-stage dialectic that would appear over two thousand years later—is itself not immune to combativeness. Let us set aside for now the question of whether this combativeness—combativeness to the point of a desire to dominate—which caused and continues to cause Plato and Hegel and all their continuators to repeatedly backslide out of philosophy and into sophism, inheres in the dialectic as such or is merely a result of its abuse. In any case, the introduction of the dialectic, in the framework of which the discovery of contradiction was converted from a means of contesting the truth to a means of working towards it, did not safeguard against every possible abuse of contradiction.

In spite of the dialectic, the overcoming of sophism by philosophy is a task that still remains to be realized. What Plato believed he could decry as merely an abuse of dialectic, as in the following passage from his dialogue on the *Republic*, has in deed and truth been the fate both of his own and every other use of dialectic.

> Is not one lasting precaution not to let them have a taste of it while young? I do not think it has escaped your notice that when youths get their first taste of reasoned discourse they take it as a game and always use it to contradict. They imitate those who cross-examined them and themselves cross-examine others, rejoicing like puppies to drag along and tear to bits in argument whoever is near them.—Yes, to excess.
>
> And when they have themselves cross-examined many people and been cross-examined by many, they fall vehemently and quickly into disbelieving what they believed before. As a result, they themselves and the whole philosophy are discredited in the eyes of other men.—Very true.
>
> An older man, I said, would not want to take part in such folly; he will imitate one who is willing to converse in order to discover the truth rather than one who is merely playing and contradicting for play; he will himself be more measured and will bring honour rather than discredit to the pursuit of philosophy.[6]

Chapter 2

FORGOTTEN AND OVERBLOWN CONTRADICTION

The unity of the Middle Ages

The forgetting of contradiction and this forgotten contradiction's exaggeration during the Middle Ages are one thing, and the efforts that threaten to eradicate it in modernity are another. It can be left aside that the Middle Ages, understood as the real type of the Middle Ages, already displays modern features and that modernity, understood as the real type of modernity, continues to display medieval features. The contradiction that was forgotten by the Middle Ages—the ideal type of the Middle Ages—nonetheless remains disturbingly and destructively present as the diabolical threat of its exaggeration into a dualism. Meanwhile, the danger of modernity is that the contradiction that it—the ideal type of modernity—can never forget is subject to attempts at eradication through the repression, oppression, sabotage, postponement, and dissipation of its creative presence.

Owing to its primary focus on the connection between faith and knowledge, which had led the way out of antiquity, the Middle Ages fell behind relative to the advanced position afforded by antiquity's discovery of contradiction. The Middle Ages placed greater importance on, and derived more guidance from, its own accomplishment of connecting philosophy and theology than it did from the ancient discovery of the contradictions of thought and of faith, which led to the differentiation of philosophy from sophism and of true from false prophecy. The unity of the All thus established by the Middle Ages seemed exempt from all contradiction, all the more, or at least also, because antiquity had developed these two perceptions of the truth side by side without pressing forward to the possibilities and limits of grasping them together. Philosophical knowledge of reason on the Greek side and revealed religion on the Jewish side had already reached states of completion by the time conceptual thought and faith-bound awe encountered one another.

Modernity on the other hand could not and cannot overlook either the discovery of the contradictions in thought and faith, which emerged side by side in antiquity, or the contradictions that were, by means of the medieval synthesis, forgotten at that time, despite having made themselves heard since. What follows from these contradictions is precisely the calling into question of every unity, and it has made modernity into a fundamentally new era, an unprecedented age of freedom. To be sure, the diversity of contradictions in modernity impacts its freedom and should not be underestimated, but neither should the freedom the Middle Ages had already attained be underrated. That unity, which, in the medieval period, was more important than the contradictions that called it into question, bestowed an almost enviable degree of freedom, but it still lacked the self-responsibility on whose unconditional initiation modernity is founded.

The paradigm was still the circle, the supposedly most perfect shape according also to ancient tradition, and its respective center remained determinative. Obstructing every mutual encounter was this one-and-only center by which each and every participant was assigned its place in the encounter and held responsible for its realization of truth. The commandment of neighborly love was not for the neighbor's sake, but for God's. The commandments "Love your fellow as yourself" (Lev. 19:18) and "The stranger who resides with you shall be to you as one of your citizens; you shall love him as yourself" (19:34) are expressly founded in this way: "I am the Lord (19:18)—I the Lord am your God" (19:34).[1]

Because the circle only ever has a single center—unlike the ellipse, whose no less perfect shape, with its two focal points, is paradigmatic for modernity—the world that turned around this center could contain contradictions, but it could not be contradictory as such. Not only China, but also "catholic" Christendom, which equated the totality of the All with its own Whole, formed a "Middle Kingdom," which, although it tolerated life beyond its own ambit, laid claim to the truth, the whole truth as such, for itself alone. That which contradicted it from the outside played a role, and an increasingly overblown one at that, but without calling into question the unity of the world that the center guaranteed and whose loving omnipotence, as Dante's final terza rima puts it, "holds sun and stars in circle's quiet union."[2]

The All of the Middle Ages

Consider the rose window of the Lausanne Cathedral with its depictions of the seasons, elements, zodiac signs, months, cardinal directions, life cycles, temperaments, rivers of paradise and fabulous creatures. They are mere fragments of all that was once included here within four roses. Or recall the abundance of figures contained in just a single medieval cathedral, or look up at the ceiling of St. Martin's Church in Zillis! In this demonstration of the truth of the 153 large fish caught by the Peter of the Gospel of John—"and though there were so many, the net was not torn" (21:11)—one's eyes must take in fifteen times seven pictures framed by a further forty-eight: 153 altogether. Fifteen rows of seven pictures each tell first the biblical story and then that of St. Martin, the embodiment, and thoroughly adequate embodiment, of all history as such, on all sides contained by the ocean evoked by the images of the frame. Here, animals are transformed into humans and the behemoth reigns, setting limits, impassable limits, for the human being. Only the crucifix that is worked through the entire ceiling connects the beyond of these fabulous creatures with the here of the remaining All.

So there certainly is contradiction, but not as contradiction of the whole of one's own world, despite the fact that one's own here and beyond by no means encompasses everything. That other worlds perceived the same center differently, or perhaps even turned on an altogether different center, was only dimly available to consciousness and therefore incapable of calling one's own world into question. There was the Jew for example, who, even with his biblical past, was included in the "catholic" whole as the bearer not of his own prehistory but that of Christendom. The postbiblical continuation of Jewish life, and the Jew's contemporary presence, which he was still able to master in visible and creative ways, was thus not taken seriously and considered as part of the whole. And in a similar way, Islam and the incalculably diverse paganisms of Asia and Africa only ever counted as the nearer or further margins of one's own ambit, without ever amounting to an essential contradiction.

As late as 1928, a thinker of the likes of Peter Wust could conclude his *Dialektik des Geistes* [*Dialectic of Spirit*] with reference to a passage in Augustine in which this medieval forgetfulness of contradiction is expressed in a way that is not only touching, but also appallingly self-righteous; as if contradiction served, as Augustine had so to speak "innocently" assumed a millennium and a half previously, only to glorify his own ambit without thereby also—as in modernity—challenging it. "Miraculous wisdom," Wust says, can "be contemplated with wonder in the entire objective-phenomenological architecture of history [...] Even the negative in history, with all its downward-driving weight of destiny, sets positive forces free which bring about good where evil had been intended or where only imperfection had been achieved."[3] And it is at work everywhere, truly everywhere, as one can read on Wust's last page, the whole of the All in the guise of "eternal dialectics" demonstrating the truth and only ever again demonstrating the truth: "*all* negativity's wonderful power of manifestation."[4] And so it came to pass that on 24 August 410, Augustine and his church were called fundamentally into question when the unthinkable, which should have been entirely excluded from possibility, nonetheless happened: Alaric's pillage of Christian Rome. Christendom's own center, in its eyes the focal point that bore and guaranteed the consistency not only of its surroundings but also of the entire All, had been conquered by an enemy that really existed after all, and with a power superior to that of its own world.

> For God would never have created a man, let alone an angel in the foreknowledge of his future evil state, if he had not known at the same time he would put such creatures to good use, and thus enrich the course of the world history by the kind of antithesis which gives beauty to a poem. "Antithesis" provides the most attractive figures in literary composition: the Latin equivalent is "opposition," or, more accurately, "contra-position." The Apostle Paul makes elegant use of antithesis in developing a passage in the Second Epistle of the Corinthians.

Here Augustine gives examples from Paul (2 Cor. 6:7 et seq.) and Ben Sira (33:15):

> The opposition of such contraries gives an added beauty to speech; and in the same way there is beauty in the composition of the world's history of arising from the antithesis of contraries—a kind of eloquence in events, instead of in words.[5]

The anxiety of the Middle Ages

The consequence of the forgotten contradiction of the Middle Ages, and of every modern continuation of the Middle Ages, is that contradiction is exaggerated into the dualism of the irreconcilability of two world powers, with the ultimately only good on one side and the perpetually only evil on the other. As devil, heretic, witch, Jew or—of late—migrant worker, the Completely Other forgotten by consciousness remains the terror of a universe prematurely closed off by this consciousness, only to find its own universe the more fully exposed to contradiction.

Along with the "beauty of the All"—in whose ambit the here and the beyond are able to assume a form, as we saw on the rose of Lausanne or the ceiling at Zillis and from Augustine to Wust, with their overwhelming abundance of truths of faith and knowledge and their wealth of mutual tensions—goes the anxiety of being literally confined by the foreigner who is not included in one's own universe, despite his or her very real presence and existence. It is an anxiety that arises in the face of everything and everyone with whom this All does not come to terms, but does, to its horror, collide! Despite the premature objections of some, there is no danger of dualism for a worldview that, informed by the modern breakthrough to dialogic, reckons with contradiction; dualism was and remains, rather, the danger of every medieval worldview that forgets to reckon with contradiction.

Where contradictions are reckoned with, the All indeed splits into fundamentally different, even irreconcilable perceptions of its totality, but without therefore falling apart into a dichotomy. This only happens when one's own ambit is imagined as perceiving absolutely everything and is, without really perceiving everything, exposed to what it cannot perceive as if to a second truth: an evil counter-truth. A world like that of antiquity was therefore largely spared this dualism, even though it never became conscious of the full extent of the diversity of contradictions in the universe, because it drew its own limits and recognized an Other and Completely Other beyond its own reach. So long as humans accepted the gods and the fate that governed them and everything else as a beyond counterpoised to every here—which meant they had to reckon with this beyond wherever they were and whatever they did—they were safe from the horror of dualistic division. They were spared the fear of an other which was on the one hand excluded, but on the other hand impossible to exclude.

It is only the unaccepted beyond that, to the extent that it is not accepted, yet present, induces the horror of confinement that is characteristic of dualism and marks it as a dead end: like a lingering fear that has not been understood and therefore continues to erupt with ever greater intensity.

When, at the height of its unification of faith and knowledge, the Middle Ages went beyond antiquity to henceforth hold the here and the beyond in a single embrace, its universe was no longer subject to limitations. Heaven and earth and hell, that is to say everything without exception, revolved around the center of a universe that was accessible, in part by revelation and in part by reason, to the outermost reaches of its ambit. And it seemed as if everything had to revolve around this center if for no other reason than that a circle can only ever have a single center. But this was also dualism's undoing. If the Other and Completely Other nonetheless existed, calling one's own All fundamentally into question, this counterpart could only have arisen from the ambit of a different center-point. Precisely because one's own world was supposed to constitute the entire world, there existed not only its All, which had to be reckoned with, but also confinement owing to counterworlds of the most terrifying incalculability: fear-inducing, diabolical otherness everywhere.

That this dualism then bespeaks a battle of one's own world with this second world, vis-à-vis which one's own truth must finally emerge as the only truth, but only after a long, very long time—up to the very end—during which the counter-world (whose so-called truth is a lie and nothing but a lie) will have nonetheless reigned supreme, does not demonstrate any insight into the fundamental reality of contradiction's being. It proves, rather, a mere lack of insight with regard to it.

To be flooded in this way by contradiction that has become overblown by being forgotten is one thing; to reckon with the fact of its existence is another.

A counterpart with which one reckons as such, that is to say, as an other capable of contradiction, evokes at worst only such fear as knows what it fears, and against which it can therefore also defend itself. That anxiety, however, which to its horror does not know what is confining it, intensifies, in attempting to defend itself against this unknown, into ever greater anxiety and finally into a panic of literally deranged fear: frightened, confused flight towards that which fear fears. Thus dualism also botches this step, whose occasion—unrecognized occasion—is contradiction. Forgotten and overblown contradiction becomes visible as the fear of the Completely Other who should not exist and yet does, while still remaining invisible to the victim of this fear. So long as the human being remains under the spell of fear, it does not get and never can get to the bottom of precisely what it fears.

Only the setting free of contradiction liberates from dualism and from its anxiety. Its price, its unavoidable price, is the end of the Middle Ages.

The end of the Middle Ages

"Now, it is important to be able to attach oneself firmly to [the doctrine of] the conjunction-of-opposites," declared Nicholas of Cusa in the year 1458.[6] But he falls right back into the Middle Ages when he adds the following, which might well have come from Augustine: If "you are puzzled [...] why is there in the perceptible world so much contrariety? You are to reply: 'because opposites juxtaposed to each other are more elucidating, and because there is a single knowledge of both.'"[7]

Between those two sentences however is a third one that Augustine did not express, and never would have expressed, a bold, path-breaking proposition for modernity that leaves the Middle Ages behind. The conjunction-of-opposites constitutes, Cusa says, "a vision that already carries complete certainty within itself." The back-and-forth of opposites is not a faltering that necessarily entails the danger of stumbling and of looking for a hold to avoid stumbling. The "conjunction-of-opposites—a vision that already carries complete certainty within itself"—is rather self-grounded, in itself a sufficiently stable foundation.

As soon as opposites existed which could no longer be traced back to a commonly held certainty, but instead already represented complete certainty in the form of oppositional conjunction—such as the Book of Nature when faced with books (such as the Jewish Torah, the Christian Bible, and the Islamic Qur'an) or like philosophy when faced with theology, the state when faced with the church and individuality when faced with other individuals and society—the death knell of the Middle Ages had sounded. It was not yet possible to suspect that this vision—of opposites that could never be unified, but which must in future be sustained "firmly" without faltering—had merely scratched the surface of the tensions that would henceforth have to be reckoned with. The diversity of the All's contradictions, which cannot be contained in any opposition, but which lead instead into a reality of far greater tensions, had in this way just been discovered anew.

Chapter 3

REPRESSION OF CONTRADICTION

From opposition to contradiction

Opposition and contradiction are two different things. Opposition is the Either-Or of the "alternative" or alternation; contradiction is the Either-And-Or of conflict: a collision.

The opposites of an opposition exclude each other precisely to the extent that they complement each other. Such that for each opposite, the opposite facing it is beyond consideration; but the one whole, embodied by the mutual exclusivity of the opposites together, remains visible all the way into the Either-Or of their alternation. White and black, good and evil, young and old are thus oppositions, that is to say, as Either-Or they also constitute a common whole: the unity of an opposition. Every opposite remains dependent upon the other opposite: without darkness there would not even be light, just as there would be no good without evil and no old age, were there not also youth.

But when people of differing skin color or good and evil people or young and old people encounter each other, each of them could, in their independence, enjoy life without its respective other; but life nonetheless cannot live on in ignorance of the fact that the All—on the grounds of modernity—encompasses all of them together. Rather than merely alternating with each other, they embody an Either-And-Or; not as a common whole, but as a dual whole, that is to say, as something mutually contradictory: a collision. The white person and the black person, like the good and the evil or the young and the old person, are simultaneously present without being conditioned in their mutually independent existences by the existence of their other: an existence that one's own being calls into question to the same extent that it finds itself called into question by the being of the other.

The contradiction that erupts from opposite skin colors does not constitute a truly necessary collision, however. For historical and other reasons that are merely superficial (but not therefore any less real), this collision has come to weigh heavily on our time. While the example of this collision can on the one hand hardly be taken seriously enough, it points on the other hand towards a contradiction that could conceivably be overcome; doing so remains a goal to be fought for with complete and utmost resoluteness.

It is much more unavoidable, however, that good should see itself called just as fundamentally into question by evil as evil is by good. It is true that every single person is also a world of opposition between good and evil, that is to say—in essence—good as well as evil, and one or the other by virtue of each respective deed. But together, people do not constitute a common whole that is both good and evil, nor do they realize one or the other in alternation. They constitute rather—on the grounds of their common universe—collisions between what are always two whole persons, of whom, in contradiction to one another, one is better and one more evil than his or her counterpart.

The same collision—which can never be unified, for it is fundamentally irreconcilable—occurs when a young person and an old person encounter each other. It is not that one and the same person, being either young or old, in both instances unites within him- or herself youth and age, which, despite excluding each other, also make him or her into a singular, whole person pulled in both directions by the tension of the opposition; rather, what we find are two different people contradicting each other, one in youth and one in old age.

> I swear, old age is like a frigid fever,
> Of aches and shakes and crotchets bred.
> One who is thirty years or over
> Already is as good as dead.
> It would be best if you were put away.

says Goethe's Baccalaureus,[1] and many an elderly person emits the same sigh in reverse in wishing they could simply bid good riddance to everyone under thirty.

In the case of the alternating opposites of an opposition, what is at stake is the tension of an Either-Or; no matter which of the two possible decisions is made, it is one and the same unity that is thereby confirmed. Furthermore, these alternating opposites are—as a decision for one way or the other—sufficient unto themselves. Contradiction, on the other hand, involves insertion into the tension of an Either-And-Or, in which the two possible decisions cannot be unified. It is therefore also never enough to have made a decision. Rather than alternating with the other decision, in contradiction one decision collides with the other, and each calls, with the equal weight of an entire reality, its coexistent and copresent [*mitgegenwärtig*] other irreconcilably into question.

Aristotle could still teach the impossibility of predicating something and its negation simultaneously of one and the same thing.[2] But now, one must expect to encounter various predications and their negations simultaneously; otherwise, something must have been forgotten or cleared away: the very something required for bringing truth fully to expression. Aristotle's doctrine of contradiction, according to which only that is true which includes no contradiction, does maintain its validity in relation to every individual perception and is thus always and everywhere valid in so far as, in a given moment, a being can only have a single perception. But this momentary exclusion of contradiction loses its validity in view of the All of the totality of perceptions. Henceforth, two perceptions are required to make the Whole, even though each momentary aspect [*Augenblick*] contradicts the other.

The exclusion of contradiction, which is the law of every perception in the Whole of the All, has in this future—on the grounds of modernity—ceased to be the law of the perception of the Whole.

From Hegel to Marx and Kierkegaard

"Ever since Hegel lit the dialectical fire (the auto-da-fé of previous philosophy)," Franz von Baader writes in 1822, "there is no other way than that of allowing oneself to incur its blessing, that is, by taking oneself and one's works through this fire, not by attempting to abstract from it or ignore it."[3] And indeed: although not for the first time, but in a new and revolutionary way, the dialectic surpasses every previous philosophy and takes a step forward that every future philosophy will have to catch up with, and about which—a century and a half later—the only complaint can be that it did not go even further.

This same Hegelian "second-stage" dialectic, which grasps in historical succession the collision of contradictions that Plato's "first-stage" dialectic had grasped in synchronic juxtaposition, thereby guides the contradictions in the direction of progress to the goal of their sublation.[4] Whereas the platonic dialogue's search for truth must always be repeated anew until the emerging contradictions finally prove the dialectician correct—Plato in the mantle of Socrates—Hegel's world-historical *Phenomenology of Spirit* tolerates no repetition in its progression to the new. Ultimately, however, when the totality of contradictions will have had its say, here too the final continuation of all previous theses and antitheses is imagined not as merely one more thesis to be contradicted by an antithesis; it will, rather, bring to expression a final synthesis: that concluding sublation of every previous contradiction which its dialectician had been counting on since the beginning.

It is as if Hegel's line would round itself out into a circle rather than—here in the modern sense, rather than again that of the Middle Ages—lead beyond the circle to the ellipse. As it was for his opponent Schopenhauer, who in his ahistorical fashion praised the circle as the "true symbol of nature,"[5] as the figure of that return through which alone a permanent existence became possible in the restless flow of time and its contents, nature is for Hegel, like philosophy itself, despite its historicity, "*round* in itself, like the universe": round as a circle. "There is neither first nor last, rather all is carried and held together, *reciprocally* and at *once*," he announced in the address inaugurating his professorship of philosophy at the University of Berlin on October 22, 1818.[6] And in his *Aesthetics*, carried away by the curvature of a column, he said: "The circle is the simplest, firmly enclosed, intelligibly determinate, and most regular line."[7] Although the setting free of contradiction had been elevated to the level of a maxim, at the same time, the diversity of contradictions—in view of the end of history posited by Hegel himself—was ultimately also repressed.

But first, Hegel's "dialectical fire" would incinerate all the certainties of the Middle Ages and with them all previous philosophy. This dialectic not only returns to the contradictions already discovered by Greek philosophy, it also keeps faith with the medieval unification of philosophy and theology. The world of history in which Hegel anchors Plato's dialectic is derived from the faith and the contradictions of faith discovered by biblical Jewry. Taking up these, too, Hegel adds to them—and to the contradictoriness of philosophizing—the contradiction between faith and knowledge, which Jewish and Greek antiquities, in developing side by side but separately from one another, did not perceive and which the Middle Ages, overwhelmed by the new momentum of its unification of reason with revelation, had forgotten.

But with this very same dialectic which liberates to contradiction, Hegel simultaneously repressed contradiction by positing his so-called "progress of the consciousness of freedom"[8] as the goal of the sublation of all contradictions. If the ultimate point was not the contradictory nature of the universe, but rather its overcoming, what mattered in the end was not the freedom to which every being has a claim and which is guaranteed every being by contradiction set free. What mattered instead was a goal for whose sake contradiction, and ultimately freedom, had once again been cleared out of the way. This goal already justified its dialectician in ignoring the challenging questions that, from within history's trajectory towards its goal, were reminding the present of its responsibility in the here and now. It was already possible, or so it seemed, and therefore also imperative, to ignore what was mutually contradictory in perceptions of the truth.

Grasping Plato's synchronic juxtaposition of contradictions as a series of contradictions, the succession of which is and constitutes history, Hegel did not merely detach his present from the past. The series of contradictions leading out of the past and into the present also precipitates the outcome of an incipient future that is only just emerging in contradiction to the present. With this future before his eyes, such as it should have been already deducible from the past and the present, Hegel represses the present with the very same dialectic by which he had detached the present from the past, thereby giving priority to the future. Once the totality of contradictions has intervened in history, which is now possible, or soon will be, and already was possible, at least in principle, for the contemplating spirit, the future of the sublation of these contradictions, according to Hegel, begins. Now—or soon—we will experience the unambiguous completion of the historical All, without ever again being challenged by contradiction or challenged to contradict.

But does completeness in the consciousness of freedom really set you free? asked Karl Marx in the generation after Hegel. Does the "thought process," quite correctly imagined by Hegel as a path to freedom, really capture the whole of reality? Or is this reality, whose freedom remains spiritual freedom, not in fact standing on its head? Doesn't the "Ideal" need to be translated into and transposed into the "Material," which, despite also being intended by the development of spirit, is not achieved by it?[9] Having only just been uttered, Hegel's concluding synthesis was hereby recognized as just another thesis and called fundamentally into question.

3. Repression of Contradiction

Despite being the crowning edifice of all previous "progress in the consciousness of freedom" and thus also indeed the sublation of all previous contradictions, this accomplishment of Hegel's, Marx correctly says, had succeeded neither in achieving full freedom nor in overcoming all contradictions without remainder.

The historical contradiction first brought to consciousness by Hegel, which ushers in freedom by way of thesis, antithesis, and continuation, remained superior to the first attempt—likewise Hegel's very own—to eradicate it. Hegel's liberation *to* contradiction was equaled by his repression of contradiction, but this did not prevent further attempts of the same kind. Marx and Kierkegaard—two great examples of contradiction's enduring ability to make history after, thanks to, and against Hegel—nevertheless did not stop at this outpost of liberation-to-contradiction, which their antithesis allotted to them. Instead, they succumbed to their own ways of trying to conclude by repressing contradiction.

Marx called his method the "direct opposite" of Hegel's dialectical method, but without sensing he was, if not making the same mistake as Hegel, nonetheless succumbing to the same problem in a different way, with his teleology that likewise turned around a single center. "It must be turned"—Hegel's method—"right side up again, if you would discover the rational kernel within the mystical shell."[10]

But just as Hegel's greatness cannot be called into question on the grounds that his leap forward did not go far enough, it is no challenge to Marx's greatness if the materialism with which he called Hegel's Idealism into question must also be contradicted as just another "ism." It is in part true, and in part it remains inspiring how, on Marx's view, history serves the progress of material being and not only that of ideal consciousness. But on the other hand, Marx—like Hegel—uses the very same dialectic by which he clears a path for his own contradiction (which had been ignored by his counterpart) to repress contradiction as such. It is this contradiction that, on the grounds of modernity, calls into question every teleology that claims the truth for itself alone, including the teleology of Marx.

And just as contradiction had been repressed by Hegel and Marx, so it was also repressed by the theistic existentialism of Søren Kierkegaard and the "dialectical theology" that picked up from him; and so it was also repressed by the reversal of that "dialectical theology" in the atheistic existentialism of Martin Heidegger, after both existentialisms had taken up the cause of individual truth and of putting it to the test in the life of every human being, in contradiction to the supra-individual systems of Hegel and Marx. Once again, the dialectical method served not only its practitioners themselves, in the sense that the individual they put forward was always, each as its own being [*Dasein*], justified either before or without God; it also served to turn their opponent "inside out," as if universal historicity had no claim whatsoever. But because the universality of Hegel's ideal consciousness and of Marx's material being is always also the consciousness and being of a singular existence, and because every existence is essentially distinct from every other existence, this truth too is nonetheless not the truth as such.

Only the mutually contradictory demonstrations of the truth of the particularity of every single individual and of the supra-individual universality of their history together are true, just as the ideal and material teleology of history or, in the case of existentialism, its theism and atheism together are true. Only the And of their Either-And-Or opens the whole truth—and it does so only when they contradict each other, and only so long as they continue contradicting each other.

Mao Zedong's contradiction set free

In Mao Zedong, an advocate has appeared of the contradiction rediscovered and asserted by Hegel on the grounds of modernity, as well as a critic of those attempted repressions of liberated contradiction that also go back to Hegel. With great clarity he demonstrates how, since Hegel and thereafter in the works of Marx, Engels, Lenin, and Stalin, the dialectic has acknowledged the rightful place of contradiction but has also succumbed to attempts to repress it.

What is the reason for this repression? Who is at fault? According to Mao Zedong, the reason can certainly not be found in the dialectic as such. No fault can be ascribed to it. The dialectic and the essential achievement of the dialectic, its liberation *to* contradiction, can be thoroughly secured against the repressions of contradiction. This is because it is possible, according to Mao Zedong, to remain faithful to the dialectic while also staying true to freedom.

> Without contradiction nothing would exist.[11] [...] [P]ositive and negative numbers in mathematics; action and reaction in mechanics; positive and negative electricity in physics; dissociation and combination in chemistry [...] classes and class struggle, in social science; offence and defence in military science, idealism and materialism, the metaphysical outlook and the dialectical outlook, in philosophy, and so on—all these are the objects of study of different branches of science precisely because each branch each has its own particular contradiction.[12]

Or elsewhere:

> To be one-sided means not to look at problems all-sidedly, for example, to understand only China but not Japan, only the Communist Party but not the Kuomintang, only the proletariat but not the bourgeoisie, only the peasants but not the landlords.[13]

As Sun Wu Tzu already knew over two thousand years ago:

> Know the enemy and know yourself, and you can fight a hundred battles with no danger of defeat.[14]

And as Wei Chengi, a man of the seventh century, taught:

> Listen to both sides and you will be enlightened, heed only one side and you will be benighted.[15]

But is contradiction thus really set free? And does this really get to the bottom of the attempts to repress it?

That Mao Zedong achieves neither is demonstrated by a further assumption he defends, albeit with a superficial qualification that does little to alter the claim's substance. Contradiction and opposition, conflict and alternative, are in his view one and the same. Although they are considered identical, Mao Zedong then goes on to split contradiction—which he supposes to be the same as opposition—into principal and secondary contradictions (because contradiction and opposition refer to quite different things, after all). But in principle, he argues, there is nonetheless no difference between them. The first words of Mao Zedong's speech *On Contradiction* from August 1937, which he would stress once more in February of 1957 in another speech *On the Correct Handling of Contradictions Among the People*, are as follows:

> The law of contradiction in things, that is the law of unity of opposites, is the basic law of materialist dialectics.[16]

And, a few pages later, again:

> The interdependence of the contradictory aspects present in all things and the struggle between these aspects determine the life of all things and push their development forward. There is nothing that does not contain contradiction; without contradiction nothing would exist.[17]

But in this way, it is opposition that has again become decisive, despite the formulaic reference to contradiction. Nature and the polarity of nature in the form of the cycle of nature, a millennia-old Chinese teaching, force history and the manifold contradictions of history—the originally biblical heralding of a breakthrough out of the cycle of nature—into the background. Taking as its departure point a primordial beginning that will never return, biblical Judaism taught that an ultimate goal was to be reached—reached only once and once and for all. How differently this sounds compared to what predominates, by way of Chinese tradition, in Mao Zedong's thought, even if he expresses it in the language of Western philosophy.

> Practice, knowledge, again practice, and again knowledge. This form repeats itself in endless cycles, and with each cycle the content of practice and knowledge rises to a higher level. Such is the whole of the dialectical-materialist theory of knowledge, and such is the dialectical-materialist theory of unity of knowing and doing.[18]

Or:

> It is always so in the world, the new displacing the old, the old being superseded by the new, the old being eliminated to make way for the new, and the new emerging out of the old.[19]

But the contradiction to be negotiated on the grounds of modernity, which has come to assert itself, along with history, against the grain of the polar oppositions of nature, is, to stay with Mao Zedong's example, youth on one side and old age on the other, youth and old age each being an entire world of its own. Here, two worlds encounter each other, neither of which can replace or displace the other, and neither of which can therefore succeed in repressing the other! It is precisely because they cannot repress each other that their encounter constitutes a collision. This real contradiction is precisely not a mere opposition of two alternating, mutually exclusive opposites that supplement each other in equal degrees to form a unity. The worlds of youth and old age do not alternate, like opposites do, on a single stage; they collide, rather, as two fundamentally complete stages of life. Each, incapable of unification, claims the same stage for itself alone: in contradiction to the other.

Mao Zedong helps himself out here with his own personally developed doctrine according to which there is always one decisive, principal contradiction accompanied by further secondary contradictions, with which he lets drop his initial proposition of the identity of contradiction and opposition. For what Mao Zedong refers to as principal contradiction is nothing other than contradiction, while what he calls secondary contradictions are not contradictions at all, but oppositions. The principal contradictions are for him antagonistic, while the secondary contradictions are not. There are thus conflicts in the case of antagonisms and alternations in the case of nonantagonisms, contradictions in the former and oppositions in the latter case. Or, to transition from opposition to contradiction, on the one hand there is the only improperly dialectical polarity of the cycle of nature and on the other hand the proper dialectic of history, which is driven not by oppositions, these secondary contradictions, but by contradictions—principal contradictions.

"[T]here is no doubt at all," he says in his speech *On Contradiction*, declaring in an apparently open, but in fact narrow-minded way—and constituting only in a very unsavory sense a continuation of all dialectics since Hegel:

> [T]here is no doubt at all that at every stage in the development of a process there is only one principal contradiction which plays the leading role. [...] Once this principal contradiction is grasped, all problems can be readily solved.[20]

This is accomplished namely—this is Mao Zedong's counsel—by immediately taking the side to which the future belongs. Because the future belongs to this side in the sense that it will ultimately defeat its adversaries without remainder.

The apprehension of the respective principal contradiction, which for Mao Zedong is the collision of bourgeoisie and proletariat, with capitalism on one side and communism on the other, should thus not allow this contradiction as such to have its say, to announce its twofold message of reciprocal questioning and responsibility. Rather, contradiction should be apprehended for the sole reason of using it to cut short the speech of one's other. Sooner or later, so goes the assumption, the other will have to fall silent. Then, however—but this can be left aside here, because regressing into the cycle of nature cannot rescue the fundamental narrow-mindedness of this historical stance—a new principal contradiction may erupt in the face of the victor of the previous principal contradiction. Then again, as always, the only goal is to end up on the winning side of the respective principal contradiction and to have the last word, all on one's own.

Yet what this amounts to is repressing contradiction in the name of contradiction. It sounded lovely when Mao Zedong quoted Wei Chengi: "Listen to both sides and you will be enlightened, heed only one side and you will be benighted."[21]

But he does not follow Wei Chengi in the sense of aiming to listen to everyone or even to—at least—two. He aims, rather, to discern the voice of the one whom, here and now, others still contradict, but whom, finally, no one anymore will contradict.

The weakness of every dialectic

It is not a bad will, capable of correction, but the dialectic itself and as such which, owing to the teleology that co-constitutes its essence, ultimately attempts to repress the contradiction to which it initially opens itself in an exemplary way. The same discovery of historical succession that leads out of the Middle Ages and beyond antiquity, overcoming forgetting in the former and in the latter overcoming the one-sidedness of the manifold contradictoriness of the All as experienced either solely by science or solely by faith, furthermore seduces to the preemption of what, following their thesis and antithesis, their synthesis is supposed to be.

It is precisely that this second-stage dialectic also succumbs again and again to a desire to dominate, no matter how veraciously its dialectician may strive to remain open. For the dialectician is convinced of the following: from the collision of contradiction, which raises a challenge and demands responsibility literally in the here and now—and to which the dialectician can thus concede only "coexistence," and that but temporarily—a new phase must emerge in the form of a consequent and ultimately final synthesis, which can, at least in principle, already be anticipated. It is thus already possible and imperative to begin reckoning with it now.

The criterion of every dialectic without exception—and the cause and actual justification for the desire to dominate evinced by every dialectician without exception—is in respect to the collision of contradiction, i.e., to the equal right of two claims to the fundamentally different existence [*Dasein*] of their thesis and antithesis, the firm conviction that one of the two sides is simultaneously in the wrong. According to the dialectician, one side is standing in the way of the future. Yet because the dialectician's claim carries the seed of the future, he or she may permit him- or herself, on the path towards the concluding final synthesis, to eradicate all the contradictions that challenge him or her and it, despite their initially—but only initially—recognized right to existence.

Such that what agitates begins to calm, and that which flows to freeze, dead and dealing death. While still in Switzerland, Bertolt Brecht noted in his *Journal* on January 6, 1948, with reference to "over there":

> [O]nce again this nation is swindling its way to a revolution by assimilation. The dialectic which stirs everything up in order to calm it down, which transforms the things in flux into something fixed, "elevates" matter into an idea, is just the bag of magic tricks for such shit-awful times. And at the same time this Germany is no longer really comprehensible without dialectics.[22]

Heidegger's view—a retrospective view on the occasion of his eightieth birthday in September 1969[23]—applies, on the contrary, not merely to a particular dialectic that provides a false sense of reassurance until a better dialectic can draw the torpor back into the flow, but to the dialectic as such: "The dialectic is the dictatorship of the question-less. Every question suffocates in its net."[24] And: "Today's Hegel renaissance—the ruling thought is difficult to rescue from the dialectical mill. The mill is running but with nothing left to grind, because the basic stance of Hegel, his Christian theological metaphysics, has been abandoned; it was only there that Hegel's dialectic was in its element, only there did it have any purchase."[25]

Heidegger does not, however, offer a way out. For the "revolution in thought which the human being is approaching" is not yet primed.[26] The time for discussing it has not yet arrived. This is to say that Heidegger—to level at him the same reproach he levels at the dialectic—sneaks past dialogic, the thoroughly primed revolution in thought whose time has come, and for which it will soon be high time. Yet Heidegger was satisfied merely to pillory the dialectic.

> Mere sagacity [*Scharfsinn*] is not the way to that which is still hidden from our thinking. The revolution in the mode of thought which the human being is approaching is not yet primed, the time for a public discussion of it not yet come. [...] The question remains whether industrial society, which is today taken to be the primary and ultimate reality—it used to be called God—can be thought at all sufficiently with the aid of the Marxist dialectic, that is to say in principle with Hegel's metaphysics. The method of dialectical mediation sneaks past the phenomena, past the essence, for instance, of modern technology.[27]

Chapter 4

ATTEMPTED DISPLACEMENT

Freedom of technology

On the one hand, technology is often allotted too much blame, including blame for—or at least complicity in—the repression, oppression, sabotage, postponement, and dissipation of contradiction by the dialectic. From totalitarianism and fascism to manipulation, futurology, and blinkered specialist idiocy, there is no limit to what technology has been held responsible for. Yet at the same time, technology is also uncritically celebrated. Lenin thus praised communism on November 21, 1920, as "Soviet power plus the electrification of the whole country."[1] Or should electric light have been invented only to illuminate the salons of a few snobs, and not, as Theodor Herzl put it in *The Jewish State* of 1896, "so that we could solve the great questions of humanity by its light"?[2] A quarter of a century before Lenin, Herzl's definition of Zionism was, like Lenin's of communism, "Judaism plus electrification," and in his case it meant electrification of the whole world in the service of humanity. Also like Lenin's definition, it was a statement of—at least initially—superb foresight.

In 1945, twenty-five years after Lenin and fifty after Herzl, the arrival of atomic "nuclearization" initiated the actual upheaval of politics by technology, which in the heyday of electrification had been only dimly foreseen. The "wonderful technical achievements,"[3] as Herzl called them and Lenin celebrated them, were indeed what made the political legacies of these men possible.

But it was nonetheless wrong, and it is still a dangerous deception, to displace the responsibilities of politics, the economy and science onto technology—even if they ally themselves with technology and technology follows their lead. To say that the electrification and nuclearization of the world enabled world revolutions in Lenin's and Herzl's sense of fruitful solutions to mankind's hitherto insoluble questions, or that this level of technology enabled an unprecedented repression, oppression, sabotage, postponement, and dissipation of contradiction, is only a half-truth. What is just as true is that technology ushers in the complete liberation of humankind. The human being of technological modernity, at the height of the diversity—and of the diversity of contradictions—accessible to him or her, is finally able to rise up against the threats to freedom, which will henceforth be completely transparent and never again be tolerable.

Technology, a no doubt acquiescent tool for every eradication of freedom anywhere it is put to such use, and from the very beginning both tool (in the productive sense of the word) on the one hand and weapon on the other, spares no one the necessity of defending oneself, with its help, against the threats to freedom that—with its help—threaten one's freedom. It makes as little sense to displace one's personal faults and the faults of others onto technology as it does to blame technology for one's own failure to resist those who are at fault. In the same vein, no good can be expected from technology if no one takes doing it into his or her own hands. Yet wherever good is accomplished and people stand up for freedom until contradiction is set free, technology reveals—and fulfills—the actual meaning and single true purpose for which humankind invented it for itself.

Freedom through technology

Technology is not discovered, but invented. It is not something given, waiting in nature to be found and merely expanded upon; rather, it goes—along with the human beings who develop it for themselves—beyond nature. Here, culture supplements nature; works supplement organic growth. Compared to the "natural" world of living beings, culture is a fundamentally different world in which life is fashioned by human ingenuity.

The human being, according to an expression of Sigmund Freud's that goes straight to the heart of the matter, is "as it were a kind of prosthetic God"[4]; with no other choice than to invent technology, which could not be found, the human being did invent it. To supplement nature, which human beings also are and always remain, depending upon it even from the highest summits of technology, they created means of unburdening, amplifying, and complementing themselves by means of prosthetics in the sense of Freud's albeit more skeptical than optimistic elevation of the human to a "prosthetic God." More disturbed by the disruptions threatening communal life at the height of cultural development than filled with confidence by the ascendancy of the communal life of this cultural development, Freud called the book containing this statement *Civilization and Its Discontents*.[5]

It is, at any rate, with prosthetics that human beings either prove the worth of their culture or else destroy it. These artificial limbs with which they are not endowed "by nature" constitute the tools of their technology, from the "textiles" of clothing to the "tectonics" of housing and the "text" of the fabric of writing—all tellingly related to the stem of the word "technology." According to the Bible, too, technology was the only thing added after the fact to long-since consummate nature, to Creation in its completed form. For the first and last time, the creator intervenes again to invent the tool clothing, which is, according to this biblical statement, the first prosthetic: "And the Lord God made garments of skin for Adam and his wife, and clothed them" (Gen. 3:21).

Clothing that can be put on and taken off like an artificial skin; the artificial cutting edge of a knife, from hand axe to razorblade, also always welcome as a weapon—which was, however, abused right away to the end of murder, despite every tendency of nature towards reciprocal mercy among members of the same species; not to mention "tamed" fire; these most ancient tools, as well as the much later wheel, are unknown to nature. The All does not present "homo faber," a creature that has broken through to the "fabrication" of its own creations and thereby become human, with a completed Creation, but with a whole that is exposed to his or her inventiveness, delivered to their bloodlust and entrusted to their responsibility. Nature thus constitutes and remains a foundation that cannot in any essential sense be overcome or replaced, but for and of which the human being, once become human, takes over direction and bears responsibility. He or she goes forth from nature to the work of culture, which in turn entails further consequences for nature—radical and cataclysmic consequences.

"Be fertile and increase; fill the earth and master it; and rule the fish of the sea, the birds of the sky, and all the living things that creep on earth" (Gen. 1:28). *Master it, rule them!* It is with only too much pleasure that this passage is often misunderstood in the sense of authoritarian and totalitarian arrogation of power. The same rapists of humankind and of the All who otherwise displace onto technology their guilt for the impending eradication of freedom would here displace onto the Bible a threat that stems once again from themselves alone. The Bible justifies none of the hubris that has twisted and continues to twist biblically commanded freedom and fruitfulness into its opposite.[6] The biblically set standard is not only, and not only blindly, a goal, but is furthermore the same standard that modernity, on its various paths, has likewise established.

From the same nineties of the nineteenth century, which, from psychoanalysis' entry into the interior of the psyche to nuclear physics' entry into the interior of matter, ushered in modernity in its actual and henceforth permanent sense, stems Louis Dollo's law of irreversibility, formulated in 1893. The same precedence of humankind over the fishes of the sea, the birds of the sky, and every living thing that moves on the earth taught by the Bible was substantiated by natural science as a precisely accurate indication of the essence of the human being. To be sure, even here and once again, every kind of irresponsibility remains possible, but it represents a human possibility again and again only because humans—and only they—are called to be effectually responsible for themselves, the earth, and everything that moves on it.

The animal is bound to the tools that it, with the help of its own body parts, "invents" as itself. It can, according to Dollo, refine them increasingly, but it can never reverse the course of development it has set with them. The human being is, on the contrary, not bound to the tools that it, with the help of artificial limbs (Freud's "prostheses"), invents to supplement its body. It can refine them increasingly and simultaneously use them or not use them, while remaining capable of reversing the development of the course—and of the development of every course—it has struck. The same human being who swims like a fish remains, flying like a bird, the same human being who is also on the go in every other direction in which living things move on the earth. For despite swimming, the human being is not a fish, and despite flying no human being is a bird. This living being remains, with every movement that it makes and in every direction in which it strikes out, free in relation to them, that is to say wholly him- or herself, a human being. Thanks to technology!

And it is, once again, freedom to which human beings give themselves access by means of technology or—thanks to technology—substantiate as their own essence and as one of the most essential litmus tests of their existence. The path from the power station of exploited natural power (such as flowing water, blowing wind, or the energy of animal and human muscles) via the power station of exploited machine power (which however remains dependent on the "nourishment" of accumulated stores of natural resources like wood, coal, oil, gas, water, as well as on "servicing" by human beings) to the power station of nuclear physics is a path of development towards freedom.

The power station of exploited natural power, for which the powers of human beings bear a heavy load, made the unwilling enslavement of human labor unavoidable. Likewise unavoidable was, during the First Industrial Revolution with its Second-level Power Station (for which the power of human beings as such no longer bore a heavy load), the "servicing" of machines by human beings, this torturous, coerced adaptation of human beings to the "inhuman" requirements of the machines. But the creation of cybernetics and automation, invented in tandem with the nuclear power station and also capable of taking over its "servicing," has set service free from slavery. In precisely the same way, they have also liberated spiritual labor from slavery, that is to say from mental exertion that is merely mechanical and not a work of freedom.

Freedom through technology constitutes not only the actual meaning and only essential purpose of technological inventions, but also the standard of development for technology as such, from the exploitation of immediately available natural sources of power, one of which is the human being itself, via the exploitation of the stores of natural resources that accumulated naturally over millennia, which are nonrenewable, to the liberation of the human being and of the All from all exploitation at the height of the Third-level Power Station.

At an already foreseeable time, it will no longer be nuclear fission, which still operates on the basis of destruction, but—according to the model of the "power station" of the sun—nuclear fusion that releases nuclear power. With it, that final source of power should become available, owing to which no other energy source would need to be exploited and potentially exhausted. And this theory of technological breakthrough and of the technological conquest of every form of exploitation already points the way for contemporary practice and all future thought and action. Even unrealized, this theoretically attained height of energy production has already—and globally—produced the cataclysmic consequences that, in 1951, Adrien Turel expressed in an unforgettable metaphor, although he was not yet able to give up the concept of "destruction" that was already waning with the superseded past:

> All great doers as well as all great creators were hitherto also great killers. Only since we have known that matter must be destroyed so that energy can be set "free" can we in future begin to master this curse of great deeds.[7]

4. Attempted Displacement

In addition to the substances of nature that human beings find in the here of the world, which emerged from a primordial time that, for them, is a beyond—such that they could and can merely exploit these stores of nature and with them themselves in their natural state—the beyond of nature's substances and the beyond of human beings themselves have now also been conquered, as the inside in the outside, vis-à-vis every outside. That which, in the same decades of the beginning twentieth century, succeeds thanks to the entry into the psychic interior by second-stage psychoanalysis (which goes back beyond the threshold of birth, at which Freud had stopped, to the threshold of conception, to include the nine prenatal months as well as the conception of the human being in the sphere of its responsibility), succeeds also, with the entry accomplished by nuclear physics into the interior of matter, in respect to the material All. This is the conquest of the generative threshold of matter: the locus from which matter such as it exists on earth, as well as suns and stars, are to be created.

An additional, simultaneous landmark of this advance to the utmost degree of freedom in the form of henceforth all-inclusive responsibility without remainder, it too a technological feat, is space travel. Human beings finally lift off from the surface of the earth to which they had hitherto been fettered, whereby they, themselves mature human beings in the age of humanity's maturity, finally conquer it as their home in a deepened, more mature way, for better or for worse! For several decades we have been able to gaze upon the earth in its complete expanse, without remainder, such that every child can survey it, more like a home than ever before: ports of entry and exit into every latitude, every altitude, and every depth. Space travel on the one hand and the path within on the other, which is tread by deep geology—mastery of which lags considerably behind, but which cannot add anything fundamentally new—and depth psychology and nuclear physics in parallel. The steward of these callings has assumed full responsibility for their entire ambit and for their every last and utmost aim; the attempt to master them will no doubt entail unforeseeable difficulties, but as an achievement it cannot be surpassed.

Technology contra freedom

If there is freedom, real freedom, there is also the abuse of freedom; only where there is no freedom is there no abuse of freedom. Conversely, the abuse of freedom always only confirms thereby again that freedom truly exists.

Precisely because the earthly All we call the world is henceforth really the entire world of the entire earth, the possibility of establishing world peace, which emerged with modernity, also makes the destruction of the world in its entirety a real possibility. Or, precisely because the human beings of the modern period are indeed all the human beings that exist, their suicide would mean the suicide of humanity, which it could not yet become so long as the so-called humanities of the not yet completely discovered earth encompassed mere fragments of humanity. This is the precise and sole reason why the suicide of humanity is a future possibility: because the communal life of humanity as humanity is also a future possibility that holds greater promise than ever before.

The wealth of some is no longer, as Adrien Turel recognized in path-breaking fashion, the poverty of the others. For, as he added, "Today (1955) it is already possible to say: my wealth is the buying power of the others."[8]

Thanks to the technology of the Third-level Power Station, at the height of the Second Industrial Revolution it is finally possible to still the hunger of all living human beings, and of even more human beings than are now living, all at the same time. No one must go hungry so that another can be sated. The deprivation and struggle of some for the pleasure and enjoyment of others—this immutably bitter and evil necessity of all earthly pasts owing to the technological impossibility of producing enough—is no longer necessary. But instead of excluding the possibility of future inequality, this opportunity for all human beings to be wealthy together includes the possibility that they will withhold from one another, because of greediness or other reasons, the future wealth, though sufficient for all, and become murderers rather than brothers, and worse murderers than ever before: namely murderers without necessity.

There is furthermore the threat of technology becoming an independent force, which is likewise an expression of freedom through technology, although, or rather precisely because, this autonomy can easily be turned against freedom, so as to endanger itself and others. The danger lies in the excessive grinding of technology's gears for its own sake, and an even greater danger lies in the threat of technology overpowering the technologically liberated human being to the point that every freedom, all fertility, and even humanity itself are annihilated!

A question that remains to be considered, but nonetheless passed over here, because it concerns the dangers that arise from the very freedom owed to technology, is the question of the substantial responsibility shared by science, the economy, and politics. Were it not for the goals they set, and which have taken control of technology, technology itself would be much easier to rein in. But there is also a danger, stemming from technology itself, of its tools going wild in the hands of its apprentices, as Goethe's poem *The Sorcerer's Apprentice* of 1797—as the First Industrial Revolution was only just beginning—already clearly foresaw. These apprentices of humanity can see neither the long and arduous road of invention nor the narrow path of careful experimentation, but only what technology—in the hands of the master—can accomplish.

> I marked his words and works
> And likewise their use,
> Now with spirit's power
> I work wonders too.
>
> Seine Wort' und Werke
> Merkt ich und den Brauch,
> Und mit Geistesstärke
> Tu ich Wunder auch.[9]

4. Attempted Displacement

Thus arises the threatening possibility of the unforeseeable abuse of technology in the hands of an incompetent apprentice. But Goethe's justifiably often-cited line about the extreme desperation of the apprentice who cannot rid himself of the spirits he has invoked is not his last word. It should also be remembered that the spirits invoked by the apprentice are successfully dispelled.

> For as spirits
> You are called forth to this purpose
> By the old master, no one else.
>
> Denn als Geister
> Ruft euch nur, zu diesem Zwecke,
> Erst hervor der alte Meister.[10]

Let these "spirits" of a technology broken loose mock their apprentices, too, and oppress them, and ultimately enslave them more cruelly than any human being ever was enslaved so long as slaves still by necessity existed because the Third-level Power Station did not yet exist! These "spirits" are creations of the human spirit and nothing more. Perhaps such "spirits" as emerge from science, the economy, and politics are also less the outgrowths of abused technology than the result of a different abuse that only indirectly entails the abuse of technology as well. For they too have no life of their own at bottom, but only ever that of the human beings by whom they have been called into being, a life of nonetheless immense desperation. One who would try to subdue them without having seen through them only delivers oneself—like Goethe's sorcerer's apprentice—to them once again, as if it were "spirits" that mattered and not the one who invokes them. Only when human beings stand by the fact that it was they who did and continue to do that which they lament and denounce as the fault of technology, that is to say: only when they see through the "spirits" and acknowledge them as tools and their own tools at that, can they succeed in following the example of Goethe's old master and put them in their place.

> In the corner,
> Broomsticks! Broomsticks!
> That will be all.
>
> In die Ecke,
> Besen! Besen!
> Seid's gewesen.[11]

More dangerous, then, much more dangerous than any abuse of technology—which constitutes and remains the dark side of bright possibilities—is failing to see through technology: when the human beings who invented it to serve their own needs fail to take responsibility for it. The fact that an understanding of the world advanced enough to grasp its own conception and all other inventions must face, at the height of its real responsibility for these foundational thresholds, the temptation to seize control of the psychic and material All in ways directed against freedom, should not lead to an exaggerated notion of the wickedness of technology or of the inadequacy of freedom. Technology represents a fundamental human potential that is as unavoidable as it is essential, and without its complete development human beings would not be more, but only less free, and not the complete human beings as which they are also capable of recognizing and reining in the abuse of technology.

Freedom contra technology

Once again, it is more productive and sensible to accept a contradiction than to look behind it for fault and try to displace this fault onto technology. Including the responsibility for technology, none of the essential responsibilities of the human being can be revoked without also revoking the existence of the human being, an inventor, "as it were a kind of prosthetic God."[12] That human beings are not only creatures of nature, and not only the discoverers of what they find waiting for them in nature, cannot be changed; nor can it be changed that with every new invention, its abuse is invented along with it. Only a parable, but a nonetheless instructive image is offered by the biblical description of the condition in which the human being at the height of technology overcomes the self-destructive danger stemming from technology—thanks to the same technology that enables its self-destruction. "Nation shall not take up sword against nation; they shall never again know war." For: "They shall beat their swords into plowshares and their spears into pruning hooks" (Isa. 2:4; Mic. 4:3).

Technology is necessary to the last, to heal the wounds it causes as well as for healing as such. Peace, too, requires tools, that is to say technology, but it steers technology and the freedom it promises—along with the contradictions that arise with it—onto fertile paths.

Chapter 5

ATTEMPTED OPPRESSION

The completeness of the modern world

That contradiction concerns something new—new in the sense of our modernity—is not least manifest in the culpability that, on the grounds of modernity, is to be ascribed for every attempt to eradicate contradiction. In doing so, we are no longer lamenting mere failures of omission. The days of ancient and medieval innocence belong to the past.

When the tyranny of the Greeks or the dictatorship of the Romans oppressed contradiction; when pagan seers or Jewish prophets summoned the future against the manifold contradictions of their present; and when a Christian or Chinese "Middle Kingdom" demonized its other, by whom it was, in place of the repressed contradiction, nonetheless still called into question as something Completely Other; these attempts to eradicate contradiction took place within an ambit that was not yet the complete ambit of the All. On the grounds of modernity, however, one's own and everyone's own ambit is nothing less than the complete All in its entirety.

Every future assertion of truth claiming to be the only truth will thus be proven valid in regard to its own part of the earth. But it will also be shown to be a perception that does not represent the entire earth, because it is contradicted by the truth of another part of the earth, which constitutes a valid assertion in its own right. Failing to recognize these contradictory claims to truth, each of which demands the same freedom for the truth of its own contradiction, and instead perceiving the All as if it contained no contradiction, to the end of dominating the world in its entirety, is nothing but totalitarianism: arrogation of totality [*Ganzheits-Anmaßung*] in German, in the word's modern connotation of grievous fault and blatant injustice.

In trying to find a new entryway to already familiar India, Columbus discovered a new world: unknown America. The world of his own that he had, on the grounds of the Middle Ages, taken for the entire world, proved to be a mere part of the world within its greater whole. Yet every Columbus who goes looking for an unknown America on the grounds of modernity—whether above, upon, or beneath the earth—will always again encounter an already familiar India. For on the same earth on which it was hitherto possible to take parts of the whole for the whole itself, it has become henceforth impossible to take a part for the whole and to perceive the whole otherwise than in one of its parts, alongside an other part that contradicts it.

And yet, as some will object, what about the still far from completely circumnavigated worlds and possible worlds constituted by the human being's unforeseeably numerous realms of science and of faith, to say nothing of the advances in space travel and deep geology that have hardly just begun? Do they not point to a beyond in which unification would be possible, the here of which, as it still now appears, would then represent a merely transitional diversity? Could there not be, as was already repeatedly the case, numerous, even countless unknown realms and areas yet to be discovered, and above all their center—which would then ultimately overcome the manifold contradictoriness of the All, which appears to be inescapable on the grounds of modernity?

But this is precisely the way a mature person is challenged by a young person as soon as the former—now an adult—begins to put down roots in the world, instead of setting off again and again for new conquests. Maturing youths are right in their way; they must and should remain open to all countries, professions, and life partners for as long as possible, trying themselves anew in unexplored directions. One day, however—and in this the youth is wrong vis-à-vis the adult—a fundamentally different and fundamentally ultimate step must be ventured. It is now no longer enough to merely move on; for the adult, doing so would mean fleeing from the challenge that is calling him or her to account. What comes into force now instead is the insight that one has come far enough to decide on a place as one's home, a profession as one's work, and a companion as one's life partner—in the spirit of a permanent decision.

Let other countries and professions and potential life partners and all the other unknowns entice as they may! As was hitherto the case for the human individual with its capacity for becoming an adult, the whole of the All, which once had to be discovered progressively in succession [*nacheinander*], has led humankind into a new condition of being-all-together [*Miteinander*] in the All's complete disclosedness—despite the personal immaturity initiated anew in every newborn human, and despite the fact that the maturity of humanity may now even seem to relieve the individual of the necessity of entering adulthood him- or herself.

Deciding once and for all, in the face of the whole of the All, for this way or that constitutes neither the stagnation criticized by the budding youth nor a mere reprieve, after which one would, sooner or later, set off again for new worlds. Rather, it represents the achievement of maturity, a "progressive" step forward in every sense of the word. Being responsive to the fact that there is a real and ultimate collision between decisions that call each other reciprocally into question and hold one accountable only leads further. In accepting the unavoidable reality of reciprocally contradictory decisions, adulthood does not come to a standstill but rather tests and ensures in precisely this way the completeness of the All that lies before it. It is joyfully creative in a fundamentally new way.

5. Attempted Oppression

Totalitarian arrogation of totality

The extent to which the All of modernity is in principle already completely accessible, making misdeeds of deeds that, although they had no less horrible effects in earlier times, were formerly perpetrated without the culpability that now marks them as crimes, is manifest with particular clarity in the transformation of all claims to global domination into mere totalitarian hubris. That which, until recently, not only imperialism was, but which this claim to global domination was also permitted to be—because the whole of the world had still to be brought completely into view—is henceforth nothing but totalitarianism: the claim to global domination in view of the complete accessibility of the whole of the world. It is in itself an obsolete claim: an arrogation—a criminal arrogation of totality and nothing more.

On the grounds of modernity (understood again as the ideal type of modernity, without regard for its real type or for the Middles Ages, which in various ways still persist within its frame), imperialism, this millennia-old claim to global domination, whether of faith, of knowledge, of economy or of politics, no longer exists—nor can it. Ever since these same imperialisms helped bring about the complete and permanent discovery of the entire All, any further claims to global domination made here can constitute only an arrogation of authority over this whole world, a world that is no longer off in the distance, but already present and incapable of ever again being unified.

Seven properties characterize the operative mode of totalitarianism. While these were also already characteristic of the claims to global domination of earlier periods, they have now become so unbearable that they strike us as something fundamentally new, as if they constituted what is specific to totalitarianism. But this is a misunderstanding its profiteers only welcome. For then it would not be the hubris of totalitarianism itself that would be at fault and subject to denunciation, so much as the malignance of these properties and, with them, the evil of all previous claims to global domination. But in fact and truth, it is not the means used by totalitarianism, but totalitarianism itself, and it alone, which transforms these means—which as such are certainly dangers, and capable of fault—into the particular danger and unique iniquity of oppressing contradiction in defiance of contradiction set free, and this in the very hour of its historic and irrevocable confirmation.

Some ideology glorifying its own claim to global domination in a doctrinal and apologetic way serves as a program for subsuming the masses, the individual members of which, who know better, are only first constituted as a mass by this ideology. They are then handed over to the individual will of a so-called leader [*Führer*] and a gang of his henchmen, with the help—thirdly—of a secret police force and fourthly of terror: horror for the sake of more horror, the increasingly sinister arousal of dread [*Angst*]. Fear [*Furcht*], on the other hand, which trembles in the face of something comprehensible and against which, precisely because it is comprehensible, defense is possible, unites, whereas dread only isolates. This proliferating horror separates people from one another because no one any longer demands a particular reason for it—searching for a thousand, one finds a million. And when either someone else, near or distant, or any person him- or herself is swallowed by the abyss—to which the only possible response is dread—they are already delivered to it, even before they have been snatched away, as terrified victims, into its torture chambers and, after a brief or else slowly mortifying imprisonment, ultimately destroyed for good. It almost seems less sinister, and much less terrifying, as conventional wisdom would have it, to finally meet one's demise in a terrifying end than be forced to endure that endless terror by means of which the potentate and his henchmen secure the following threefold monopoly.

Their command of information consists of complete control over communications domestically and with abroad, as well as over military armaments, that is to say over every possible use of force. The violence of the state is unhinged from the rule of law while, in reverse, all resistance against it and its rulers is denounced as injustice and furthermore exposed to the despotism of a third monopoly: the economy is controlled by being withdrawn from all public oversight and participation in decision-making. While this may be called planning, in reality it amounts to little more than plunder: an unbridled and merciless raid, in the course of which all the professions, as well as the educational tracks and courses of training leading to them, are "nationalized."

Doesn't technology play a role in this, this technology of the Third-level Power Station at the height of the Second Industrial Revolution? Isn't it precisely this technology that first enables totalitarianism as such and creates from the means of its arrogation, which have always been available, the new, modern threat to the world, in which a totalitarian leadership and its ideology and secret police with their monopoly on information, force, and economy terrify people beyond measure: more sophisticated, more extensive, and more sinister than ever before?

It must be acknowledged that the possibilities for collecting information that have emerged at the height of this technology, along with the new means of intercepting information and, in reverse, controlling the dissemination of lopsided and false news, are not a mere continuation or escalation of long-familiar processes. In addition to being intensifications of ongoing processes, they are indeed also something completely new. The same is true of the destructive force of modern weapons technology and of the modern capacity to contrive and enforce ideologies, thanks to the first steps taken into the psychic interior, which succeeded alongside those into the interior of the material All at the turn of the century. And it is also true of the modern capability to simulate planning the economy while in fact exploiting it. The extent to which the working human being can, at the height of modern technology, literally be consumed without remainder—like all the natural resources that make up the human environment—surpasses all previous harm ever done.

But to see technology as the decisive factor in what is new about totalitarianism nevertheless misses what is truly crucial, because modern technology does not only liberate hitherto unknown forces, it also signals the freedom of those who put it to use. What is new about totalitarianism—and what is thoroughly new about fascism and what is modern about manipulation, futurology, and blinkered specialist idiocy—is not to be found in any external factor, on the basis of which something in itself long-since known and familiar would take on a new face, but in the following circumstance and in it alone: Each of these attempts to eradicate contradiction falls short of modernity, for which the fact of contradiction has become, and will remain, foundational.

Fascist arrogation of force

Totalitarianism is the arrogation of totality based on an obsolete claim to *global domination*, which in spite of its obsolescence still has an air of greatness about it, if only an air of apparent greatness. For totalitarianism follows in the wake of ages in which this claim was real and had to be real, was permitted to be real. The pursuit of global domination was in the past no less brutal, but it was unavoidable—and to that extent also an act of innocence. The world, which was only first fully discovered in the process of that pursuit, was at that time not yet that entire All as which it confronts totalitarianism and decries, by virtue of its manifold contradictions, every attempt at unification as hubris.

Fascism, by contrast, is the arrogation of force based on an obsolete claim to *supremacy*, and nothing but violence and hubris, without any air of greatness.

The first denunciation of fascism, which did not yet exist in name, we owe to the brilliant diagnosis of Karl Marx's *18th Brumaire of Louis Napoleon* of 1852. As if the thievery, perjury, illegitimacy, and chaos of Bonapartism "as autocratic Executive power" could rescue property, religion, the family, and order![1] At the same time, this political movement emerges as a personal disposition towards everyday life: authoritarian as well as fascistoid.

Yet no individual who claims supremacy over his or her family, neighborhood or school, and no so-called elite, as a supremacy of the elect, has a due right to the privilege they claim, even if such privilege had at a previous time really existed in the way they imagine it—which is anyway doubtful.

In contrast to totalitarianism, which is the continuation of a superseded possibility in the hour of its impossibility, fascism involves imagining that a former possibility, which had never truly been possible in the first place, had indeed been possible. Totalitarianism builds on an obsolete—though formerly path-breaking— legality and legitimacy, whereas fascism can only ever feign the rule of any law whatsoever. The totalitarian claim to sovereignty over the whole of the world at least points from its obsolete past into the future, the whole of which, having in fact been made accessible, it opens up in a different way on the grounds of the thus transformed present. By contrast, the fascist claim to supremacy would force upon its present and future a past in which, if anything at all, only the bygone would begin again, and in actual fact nothing at all begins.

That yesterday in whose name fascists attack today and tomorrow never existed as it does in their retrospective imagination. Aside from the present and its future, which they try to undo, nothing else is possible. For the sake of an impossibility, the possible is obstructed and annihilated before it can bear any fruit.

In his *Heritage of Our Times*, Ernst Bloch grasped the murky wellspring of fascism precisely as the contradiction of non-simultaneity and denounced it with a determination that was exemplary for the year of 1935. "History is no entity advancing along a single line, in which capitalism, for instance, as the final stage, has resolved all the previous ones; but it is a *polyrhythmic and multi-spatial entity, with enough unmastered and as yet by no means revealed and resolved corners*."[2] That is to say: "Not all people exist in the same Now."[3] Those who at first glance seem to be united in the same Now constitute this simultaneity "only externally, through the fact that they can be seen today. But they are thereby not yet living at the same time with the others.[4] [...] As a merely muffled non-desire for the Now, this contradictory element is *subjectively* non-contemporaneous, as an existing remnant of earlier times in the present one *objectively* non-contemporaneous."[5]

The *subjectively* non-simultaneous, "in tranquil times [...] the peevishness or contemplativeness of the German petit bourgeois who withdrew with curses and fervour from the life in which he could not keep up,"[6] is transformed in unsettled times and under increasing impoverishment into the rebellion of "accumulated rage,"[7] at which point it also activates the *objectively* non-simultaneous. This is the "existing remnant of earlier times,"[8] all "that which is distant from and alien to the present,"[9] the "unfinished past,"[10] which, despite having been left behind long ago by the present, has still not been worked through by it. These two contradictions amplify each other: "the rebelliously crooked one of accumulated rage and the objectively alien one of surviving being and consciousness."[11]

The reciprocally amplifying contradictions of subjective-personal and objective-historical non-simultaneity transform indeed the dammed-up rage into rampant raging and degenerate from rebellious lopsidedness, leftover out-of-place-ness [*Fremdheit*], and anachronism into acts of violence whose trace almost resembles a path, and may even resemble a path to a goal. As consequential as they may prove in terms of quantity, they are nonetheless incapable of yielding quality. The essential course and progression of history remains untouched by the claims to revolution, quality, and historicity made by the contradictions of non-simultaneity; for all their stridency and forcefulness, they ultimately amount to a mere bluff.

Nonetheless, Bloch adds, considering also the other fact, often neglected in view of the apparent obsolescence and manifest fruitlessness of every fascism, *its reality exists*: "as the terrible example shows."[12] Thus Bloch, as early as May 1932, comprehends and sees through the abyss that was then opening up in Germany in place of the possible present and future: the abyss of an imaginary past impossible to realize, or of a past that may have been, but was at any rate already obsolete even before—as it is called thirty years later in the afterword to the expanded edition—the "night of 1933."[13]

And this "terrible example" of the arrogation of force based on an obsolete claim to supremacy furthermore constitutes its "subjective non-contemporaneity" not only as fascism in the sense of a political movement of "objective non-contemporaneities," but also as the fascism of personal disposition, which can form in any person at any time and burst forth as violence. Whereas totalitarianism, in continuing to pursue an historical possibility after it has become impossible, is subject to a historical criterion and can therefore—under altered historical circumstances—hardly be continued indefinitely, fascism is in essence unhistorical, that is to say, nothing less than eternal.

Fathers, mothers, teachers, indeed all adults and children who lose their grip on an authority that had never been real superiority, but only ever sheer physical strength or some other means of sustained extortion—if not merely their own fantasy of superiority—rescue themselves, as soon as their loss of authority threatens them with an insight into their inferiority, by arrogating "authoritarian" and "fascistoid" force. It is of no consequence whether they were once truly superior to the contradiction of those vis-à-vis whom they now insist on their supremacy or whether they were only so in their imagination. In the here and now of their impending inferiority, it is mere arrogance for them to insist on their supremacy and in its name permit themselves every kind of violence as if they were standing up in self-defense to protect an authentic right. Whereby they—with another characteristic move, which but again shows that their claim and behavior are nothing but hubris—brand as injustice and heresy every attempt to defend against themselves, which in contrast to their own use of force is indeed self-defense in the protection of an authentic right.

Or one may have, in reverse, been subject to an authority, which—like that of parents, teachers, and adults in general—all too often stems not from any real superiority, but only from greater age or, again, physical strength or some other external position of power, which one day pitifully collapses. If they had encountered real superiority, they would—now standing on their own two feet—now also be able to keep going on their own. But they were only at the mercy of a pretense to superiority, that is to say, oppressed: forced to repress their own strength. When such an authority collapses, those who had previously been at its mercy—who are indeed marked by it, and deeply so—find an ally in its core of authoritarianism.

Whether as this personal disposition or as a political movement, fascism oppresses contradiction in both instances, not because the meaning of this contradiction has not been—or not yet been—made clear enough to it, but because fascism is no match for this or any other contradiction it encounters. At the core of all fascism is inferiority, which ultimately condemns it to being unteachable. Trying to make it clear to fascists that their oppressed adversaries have rights of their own, and dignity at least equal to theirs, only aggravates the constantly resounding feeling and ever-present awareness of the groundlessness of their own demands, and their ethical and historical inferiority, which they try to drown out with their strident blustering. The only consequence of applying pressure to fascism is, instead of the desired dismantling, a further escalation of its pretension to supremacy and of its claim to the right to violence for itself and itself alone.

Showing fascism its own injustice only proves to it the very thing that constitutes its own point of departure, not admitting the truth of which characterizes it, which—thus aptly taken to task—can only respond to the challenge with even more insolent displays of arrogance and unbridled violence. Violence is the answer of those who are incapable of responding to that which calls them into question. It thus remains senseless to try to remind fascism of its responsibility and to quarrel with it for the sake of greater insight. Instead, the task must be to keep alive, shake up, and foster awareness of responsibility and greater insight wherever they stir, in spite of fascism—in which they never stir and never will—and in the face of it.

Not fascism, which oppresses contradiction, but the empowerment to contradiction, which fascism unjustly oppresses, is the starting point for setting contradiction free into the consciousness of everyone and of all the oppressed!

The right to contradiction as the right to resistance

Contradicting is not just one creative power among others that are capable of being forcibly oppressed, but never fully extinguished; it is, rather, and above all, also a right: one of those rights which—"when man, oppressed, has cried in vain for justice"[14]—can yet be glimpsed aloft, "for ever his." It remains, in Schiller's inspiring and sublimely true words, the "limit to the tyrants' power":[15] that the oppressed, when "each and every peaceful means [has] been tried"[16] and tried in vain, can and may take heart, reach into the heavens and pluck down for him- and herself "those rights which are for ever [theirs] / As permanent and incorruptible / As are the stars."[17]

Within this "eternal" right to resistance, which for its part constitutes a fundamental component of eternal natural right, the right to contradiction emerges likewise as an inalienable "aloft" as soon as modernity encounters the "below" constituted by the diversity of contradiction, which must be taken into account if its historical moment is to bear fruit.

Education as "an education to contradiction and resistance" is what Theodor Adorno called for in a final public statement, not three weeks before his death on August 6, 1969. "An education to contradiction and resistance," as he concluded his conversation with Hellmut Becker on *Education to Maturity* on July 16, 1969, is, or rather would be, Adorno says—for it "can in no way be taken for granted because it would still have to be established everywhere, really in every single aspect of our lives"—"the only real concretization of maturity."[18] Adorno thus connects contradiction to resistance and both to maturity, although his concern is not to demonstrate their intertwined essence or the historical necessity of their appearance. He was interested in them here only as a point of departure for settling accounts with his contemporaries.

But maturity [*Erwachsenheit*], what Adorno calls *Mündigkeit*, is more than just a criterion of contemporary reckoning. Adulthood or maturity is the immediate as well as unavoidable consequence of the completeness of the modern world, whose emblem is formed by the fully accessible totality of the All, which for its part has become the "limit to the tyrants' power" in the face of which totalitarianism's arrogation of totality and fascism's arrogation of force prove to be forms of oppression that call to be resisted and against which resistance is possible.

Whether or not the right to resistance as the right to contradiction is already coming clearly enough to expression, and above all, whether it is being articulated powerfully enough to meet resistance's call for defense, is another question. Couldn't the freedom of contradiction also serve to obstruct resistance, because words lead only to more words whose protest fails to eradicate the oppression against which they are aimed? Doesn't the contradiction that rises up against oppression simply belie the fact, precisely because it does speak out, and regardless of whether it is permitted to or not, that oppression has never yet been truly eradicated and never will be in this way?

It might be enough to insist at this point on the power, the world-moving power of the word, which is and has been forbidden, or at least never fully emancipated, by every form of oppression without exception—because the word really is capable of overturning the world—were it not for, in addition to the modern oppression of contradiction, the novelties of its dissipation at the hands of blinkered specialists, its futurological postponement, and its sabotage by manipulation. Although setting contradiction free defies the public disenfranchisement of contradiction in the forms of totalitarianism and fascism, it cannot yet be taken for granted that it will not be subject to manipulation, that is to say, that it will not succumb to surreptitious disenfranchisement. But even this and every other attempt to eradicate contradiction can do nothing at all to overturn the fact that its diversity forms the emblem of the completely accessible whole of the All and constitutes the challenging foundation of human maturity and responsibility on the grounds of modernity.

Chapter 6

ATTEMPTED ERADICATION

Attempted sabotage

Manipulation, that secret temptation under whose spell—as Herbert Marcuse expresses it—"administered" individuals come to derive satisfaction from their own mutilation, which they then continue reproducing on an enlarged scale in the belief that it is their freedom, although it remains their mutilation:[1] manipulation is the deprivation of freedom by means of its simulation. Manipulation offers contradiction a sham freedom in order to take the wind out of its sails, blocking its path to freedom yet again.

"At its most advanced stage, domination functions," says Marcuse, "as administration, and in the overdeveloped areas of mass consumption, the administered life becomes the good life of the whole, in the defense of which the opposites are united."[2] The diversity of contradictions of this whole, which are thus included in the whole despite far exceeding these oppositions—and not just their unification—, does not thereby cease to exist. On the contrary, the contradictions become charged with an increasingly dangerous explosiveness, even though they now seem in part benign and in part to have already been sufficiently expressed. The freedom offered and the dichotomous choices presented retain their contradictory nature only as a sabotaged—and that is to say manipulated—diversity of contradictions: freedom for contradiction without any real choice and without any real collision.

This way, something that ought to no longer exist survives, despite the conviction that it should not go on and is unsustainable. Public disenfranchisement at the hands of totalitarianism and fascism has been augmented by the possibility of surreptitious disenfranchisement, which now seduces people into conformity [*Gleichschaltung*]—oppressing contradiction in a way that once could have been achieved only by force—without any coercion at all, as if it were the consummation of freedom.

Instead of "delivering" the human being "from the hand" in the sense of the Latin *emancipatio*, the originally French *manipulation* covertly retains in its hand the human being who has been publicly enfranchised by emancipation on the grounds of modernity. It is no coincidence that this word only arises in the late eighteenth century. Although it perhaps began as conscientious "hand-holding," manipulation develops into increasingly unscrupulous handling, from sleight of hand to a pinch of trickery and finally to machination: instead of the good where the good had been possible, harm under the pretense of the good.

Disenfranchisement through manipulation does not arrest the immature in their immaturity. Rather, it seduces the mature into immaturity and disenfranchisement at the height of—and under the ongoing pretense of—their maturity and enfranchisement. What is new here is the element of secrecy and the possibility of its success in modernity; compared to overt, physical seduction, such as always existed and whose methods can be defended against, this sabotage from within is much more difficult to pin down, and it mocks every known defense.

But just as the oppression of contradiction in the form of totalitarianism is the mere arrogation of totality, and fascism is the mere arrogation of force—because the very diversity of contradiction they would eradicate is now constitutive of, and binding for, modernity—sabotage through manipulation now arises as their surreptitious attempt at disenfranchisement because, and precisely because, the age of maturity and enfranchisement has dawned. Although hazards have also emerged alongside emancipation on the path it blazed in breaking free to contradiction, these only reaffirm indirectly time and again contradiction's right and necessity. It is therefore a mistake to permit oneself a premature sense of security and to imagine oneself superior to the attempts to eradicate contradiction, simply because modernity is founded on the fact of contradiction's existence. But overestimating the power of the attempts to eradicate contradiction is an even greater mistake.

That same comprehensive overview of the completely discovered earth, which makes the whole All of every human being and of humankind simultaneously accessible, and seems to expose it to every encroachment and every attack, founds the diversity—and the diversity of contradiction—of humanity and of the All in a more apparent and more substantial way than ever before. Or to put it another way: the same technology used to dominate the material and psychological All, which puts into the hands of the human desire for domination never before seen opportunities for exerting influence, also opens up the possibility, at a global level, of a new human self-consciousness and of a modern consciousness of the right to freedom, which renders any attempt at domination more outrageous and unattainable than ever before.

Let the seductive tactics of advertising—the force, the overpowering force, of what Vance Packard in 1957 called *Hidden Persuaders*—spook away through the economy and politics and science and everyday life as shrewdly and deviously as they will! Wherever too much attention is demanded, attention shuts down automatically, even if the seductive flood of images and sounds can't be shut off. Ultimately, and most importantly, the possibility of Turning, which is born anew in every new human being and reemerges, despite decades of violation, in each of us after every deep sleep, is indeed still a real possibility: that possibility of Turning in view of whose renewal—and despite every lapse of whose renewal—the Jewish morning prayer dares pronounce each and every day: "The soul, that you, my God, have given me is pure."[3]

6. Attempted Eradication

As an indestructible and inalienable basis for beginning each day anew, there is the power of creative resistance by means of an imperceptible turning away from within, that is to say, inattention, as well as the power of resistance in the no less decisive form of attention: both are thresholds to Turning, no matter what a person has let him- or herself be seduced into and no matter what he or she—and humankind—is supposed to be seduced into.

Furthermore, information in the sense of neutral data and factual communication on the one hand, and its construal by interpretation on the other, are always two different things, just as leading and seducing are two different things, no matter how difficult, how nearly impossibly difficult it may be in the end to do the one without doing the other. But the insistence that leadership without seduction must be possible is itself an effect of the onset of manipulation, which—because this Either-Or does not exist—counsels self-abandonment and thus the avoidance of any trial of strength. Because all communication is already an interpretation of communication, and all leadership gives expression to superiority—which seduces, so to speak, to obedience—resistance is thought to be senseless. For we are always, and indeed everywhere, exposed to some form of manipulation.

But when it comes to communication, it makes a difference whether communicators acknowledge that they are relaying their message in their own way, which can be only partially bracketed out from the message itself, or whether they are underhandedly spinning the mediated information in a different direction than that in which the message aims and which they are publicly defending. When communicators acknowledge their role in the interpretation of the information they disseminate, they consciously take responsibility for their position, which is a necessary condition of any real encounter. But when they present as information what is in fact their own interpretation of information, they are guilty of partisanship as well as of dissimulating their partisanship: they are manipulators who sabotage the very encounter they outwardly pretend to initiate.

And there is likewise a difference, a world of difference, between leadership [*Führung*]—whose "seductions" [*Verführungen*] serve authentic authority and not just arrogated authoritarianism—that leads the led to themselves, that is to say, by leading them liberates them, and leadership that merely dissembles their liberation, if not their freedom, while in fact alienating them from themselves behind their backs. As in the case of interpretation's unavoidable entanglement in every communication, where the only interpretation guilty of manipulation is that which surreptitiously and intentionally falsifies its information, leadership is only guilty of manipulation when it is abused in order to mislead [*Verführung*].

This means, first of all, that the only seduction that constitutes manipulation is seduction against which it is possible to defend oneself and against which it makes sense to defend oneself. Because the manipulation Robert Jungk describes as a "Grasping at People"[4] is conscious and premeditated, those threatened by it are able to denounce these misleading attempts with an equal degree of consciousness and premeditation and to proceed against the guilty with every available means, including bringing them before courts of justice wherever possible.

Although manipulation remains "on the one hand a necessary part of all development," as Adolf Portmann says in much the same sense at the end of his 1969 book *Manipulation of Man as Human Destiny and Danger*,[5] he sees almost too much destiny at work, even though he also denounces and tries to defend against threats that are not fated or at least need not become our destiny. Manipulation worthy of the name, which—like collaboration—ought to be limited to instances of abuse and used as an unambiguous epithet of derision, triggers—whenever it is used as a "means of domination"—what Portmann's final sentence calls the "countermovement," by which he means: liberation to contradiction. Portmann is content to characterize it as a movement towards "critical decision-making" and to demand that all social education adopt it as its goal.[6]

Yet as soon as manipulation has to at least some extent, and in at least some of the areas in which its effects are felt, been exposed and denounced (even if it is still far from having been repelled completely), it appears again—in yet unexposed forms—in new areas, for example that of futurology.

Attempted postponement

Futurology is that preoccupation with the future as an independent sphere of inquiry which has been asserting itself in increasingly strident fashion since the middle of the twentieth century. According to its own claims, it is a new science and possibly even a foundational one, capable of synthesizing all knowledge in its totality. For a tool that is indeed new—the so-called "electron brain" of the computer—has tapped new areas of intellectual labor, enabling new means of commanding administration and every kind of control (or "cybernetics"), while also constituting a highly profitable business. The economy is only too happy to concur with this science. On the other hand, futurology's claim to ascendancy means the mere postponement of the challenge to responsibility that the diversity of contradiction presents, whether in the present or the past. With the future, and that is to say with all the futures futurology tries to predict, forecast, and dictate through planning, all contradictions without exception—which in the future will supposedly be overcome—reappear.

The concern, however, and this cannot be emphasized strongly enough, the nonetheless proper concern at the core of this new preoccupation with the future is, for the human being—for whom it is nothing new to have a future and be capable of becoming conscious of it—the fundamentally new challenge and responsibility that its modern future brings to light. Never before was there so much future to realize. And never before did acting on the future constitute so reckless an intervention, i.e., have such grave consequences beyond its mere profitability, constituting an attack against the present as well as a usurpation of the past. So long as we have no better way of understanding what it means to act on the future than the one offered by futurology, both the present, as our point of departure, and the past as its precondition are threatened with destruction.

Fully in the spirit of futurology (with which it shares the impossibility of being undone as well as the need for greater depth and sophistication), the last chapter of the first edition of Robert Jungk's 1952 book *Tomorrow Is Already Here* pays homage not only to this "grasping at the future" but also to further seizures: of supreme power, of the sky, the atom, nature, the human being, outer space, and the mind. Anyone who thinks they can simply seize what's there merely lays siege to their own present, and thereby falls back on the past, as if a future would still exist after every today and yesterday had been sacrificed to it. It has indeed—or rather, in misdeed—become possible to exterminate entire phyla and species of plant and animal life at a global level and to exhaust the material reserves produced by primordial times, just as the spiritual and intellectual treasures of all previous ages are now also being rapidly and shortsightedly wasted! All utility—even when such utility is as accessible as futurology makes it out to be—is entangled with costs for the future, in which we might now never arrive at all, precisely because it has already begun.

If only we could be certain that there is something to be gained from futurology's predictions, forecasts, and prescriptions of future utility! Yet reality, this future reality that is being undermined by the costs of its utility, also looks different from this perspective. Neither the profits for which the future is reaching nor the future itself is guaranteed simply because human beings themselves will in future do what "the future brings." The future and its utility are, rather, precisely for this reason more uncertain than ever. The increasing preoccupation with the future on the grounds of modernity does not constitute a sign of its ascertainment, penetration, or mastery but is rather the expression of its non-ascertained, unsettled, and uncontrolled nature, which will have us holding our breath from here on out. But that is not the end of futurology's confusion.

The only aspect of the future that will remain certain is so disturbing to futurology's pride in its power over the future that it fails to reckon with its arrival and is thus uncertain even of that which in fact is certain.

The future is, on the one hand, something unforeseeable that can either come to pass or not, a *futurum* (meaning "becoming" being: something still in development), and on the other hand something coming and sure to arrive, an *advent* (meaning "arriving" being: something already foreseeable as such), even if the moment of this advent's arrival cannot be determined beforehand.

From the perspective of what is immediately or eventually certainly or probably doable, or will otherwise be left undone, perhaps never to come about—de Jouvenel's "Futuribles": *futures possibles*, Jungk's models for the future, Flechtheim's futurology—it is only possible to make sense of those paths that spring from the past and, depending on the decisions of the present, run through it into the future. But the future also harbors the coming of something that will arrive no matter what, regardless of how the present and its future henceforth decide. Be it a joyful, be it an ominous advent, it will and must come: judgment of the present and of all its possible futurities, bringing with it the consequences of everything ever initiated.

No less decisive, and possibly even more ominous than the already significant danger of a utilization of the future offset by its unappraised costs—whose calculated increase in productivity could turn out to be an account of much heavier losses to its fruitfulness—is the reckoning that comes after the yesterday of all pasts, and after the today of the whole present, whose recognition has been put off until now. Guilt, like weakness and stupidity, laziness, cowardice, meanness, carelessness, and apathy, along with their effects and the countless further effects of all the other actions performed or neglected, has inescapable repercussions for a judgment that sooner or later will arrive. And on top of all that, it is a judgment that is uncannily terrifying, not only due to its largely predictable horror, but now also because of this advent's repression by futurology: for the sake of the *futurum*!

If the advent is not reckoned with—and futurology does not reckon with it, for it could not otherwise so recklessly postpone the diversity of contradiction contained in its present moment—then the fear of the future, a so-to-speak self-evident and indeed healthy fear of the impending judgment that the future represents, succumbs to anxiety in the face of this future.

Indeed, the advent comes as the guarantee of the meaning of the world and is as such a cause for joy: "your light has dawned; the Presence of the Lord has shone upon you!" (Isa. 60:1). As menacing as it is as judgment—"Go deep into the rock, bury yourselves in the ground, before the terror of the Lord" (2:10)—even the most ominous advent remains at the same time the "good news" that Jesus reads in the scroll of Isaiah in the synagogue at Nazareth (61:1, Luke 4:17ff); at the very least, it encourages Turning. But repressed, the future of this now hidden advent arouses only anxiety, deaf to every encouragement to Turning. And in its deafness, instead of daring the Turning that is open to all the guilty without exception, before every tribunal, this anxiety now faces the threat of transforming into the panic of "future shock," as Alvin Toffler has rightly been warning since 1965. Decades earlier, Adrien Turel foresaw and tried to avert the danger of this ultimately suicidal anxiety, which he called "panicitis."

A humanity that can experience nothing but terror in the face of an advent that has been repressed to the point of incomprehensibility owing to humanity's drunkenness on this *futurum*, with the help of which it—and by leaving out every advent that accompanies the *futurum*—projects for itself a superficial and false image of the world, ultimately losing control at the first sign of even the most harmless of unavoidable disappointments, hurls itself, under the spell of this anxiety, into the very abyss it so feared.

"The equids as well as the ruminants and proboscideans of the tertiary period," Turel writes in *From Altamira to Bikini, Humanity as a System of Omnipotence* [Von Altamira bis Bikini, die Menschheit als System der Allmacht], "liked to travel in unified, consolidated herds, and as a direct result of their hypertrophied cerebral intelligence they were seized with panic under the most various 'pretexts,' like a haystack going up in flames. Then these animals"—in whose "disoriented panicitis" the human being's mammalian tendency to panic is likewise rooted, shamelessly exploited again and again by the "big stock-market business and the business of war"—"stormed blindly like *one* runaway horse through a wall, then wildly off across the steppe to hurl themselves by the hundreds of thousands, like the water of the Niagara, from the steep edges of the high plains into the abyss."[7]

With this, however, which must always be recalled in order to do justice to what is fundamentally new about modernity, humankind, which in view of its future and its responsibility for the future builds—like futurology—on the *futurum* only, faces the threat of its anxiety about judgment transforming into self-destructive panic, not because humankind takes the future seriously in the way prescribed by futurology, but because, like futurology, it has not yet taken the future seriously enough.

Only at the height of the modern global upheavals, one of which is represented by each person's fundamentally new responsibility for his or her own future as nonetheless the whole future of the *futurum* and advent, can modernity be mastered. Freedom—at the summit of its contradictions, itself one of these upheavals of the world—prevails despite the old and new dangers that arise here, precisely because full responsibility has been brought within reach both inwardly and outwardly by Second-level Psychoanalysis and the technology of the Second Technological Revolution. Provided that—and there is just this one condition—human beings and humankind are firm in their insistence that in this future, there can be no Second-level Illiteracy!

Education used to be liberation from First-level Illiteracy, from the inability to read and write. But on the grounds of modernity, this now amounts to a comparative lack of education: merely being able to read and write no longer suffices at the height of the global upheavals of modernity. The only guarantee of the future is taking complete co-responsibility for the spiritual and intellectual All and for all life. Such responsibility goes all the way back—in the sense of Second-Level Psychoanalysis—to conception, in that it simultaneously—thanks to the Second Industrial Revolution—takes on an equally comprehensive responsibility for all substance, which it has learned to trace all the way back to its creation, thereby empowering itself to make its own suns and stars in the future, guaranteeing, thanks to the running start from these first beginnings, its future, with futurology and with more than futurology.

"How much of a running start does one need to jump further than one could if one were standing still?" Turel asked and answered: "In each case it is necessary that one go back to 'creation,' that one have recourse to the threshold of creation of the figure or group in question."[8] It remains true that the direction to move is forward, and it is even more possible than ever before. Precisely for this reason, however, it is also essential to stay true to one's own conditions, for they are the starting point for moving forward without neglecting one's own here and now or perhaps even losing track of it. Just as the future needs the past, which it cannot simply consume without thereby undermining itself, the present is necessary for both; without it—that is to say, if the present does not also insist on itself—the past is cut short and the future cannot dawn, no matter how objective its simulacrum may appear to be.

The present, however, and every present is, taken this seriously, either what is bad in the here and now, or, as compared to the bad, something good—and certainly a thousandfold good—that also exists, and which is, first of all, to be defended and then to be augmented if possible. But—it will be objected—doesn't the future, and that which is good in the future, get lost when—in order to press ahead to this good of the future—we proceed from what is bad in the present? And it takes so long and is so onerous to start off here and now with all the bad, in order to transform this present, sick as it is with its sickly past, into a better future! How much more quickly, as the self-praise of futurology would have it, does—or would—humanity advance, by building recklessly and uncompromisingly on what will be better in the future, with a single-minded orientation!

Nonetheless, it is not this futurological grasping at the future, which can neither take root in its own present nor trace its roots to the past (which, on the contrary, it merely attacks, exploits, plunders, and wastes), but rather a running start in the present that began in the past that, by working out the future gradually, can in fact lead beyond everything by which futurology strives for its improved future without having considered the past or assessed what the present requires.

There and only there, where the complete and unabridged diversity of contradiction—which calls to account in the present—is included from the beginning to the end, such that, in addition to what is still becoming, that which is already arriving, namely the contradiction between *futurum* and advent, which must also be sustained, is likewise foreseen; only there does that which supplements the present for the sake of replacing it and its past lead permanently beyond it, into the future!

Attempted dissipation

We need specialists, but not blinkered ones, not the positivism and scientism of science's constantly proliferating division into ever new areas of specialization. Even if this rampant division of science and its specialists is necessary, the disciplinary idiots who appear among their ranks are not. They always know more and more about less and less until finally, as the saying goes, they know everything about nothing: that is to say, they no longer realize how relatively negligible their knowledge is compared to the ambit of everything worth knowing and to the ambit of the All as such.

Experts are also conscious of the fact that they are only specialists, whereas disciplinary idiots are completely absorbed in their merely specialist knowledge: they recognize the validity of every challenge they encounter only as a question within science and, as far as possible, only within their own area of expertise, the knowledge of which, they think, is still far from being as subdivided as it ought to be. What these disciplinary idiots are attempting is the continuous dissipation of contradiction, once again as if contradiction could be eradicated on the grounds of modernity. But here as well, postponed is by no means annulled [*aufgehoben*].

In opposition to totalitarianism's and fascism's attempts to oppress contradiction, disciplinary idiocy—and hand in hand with it, futurology—indeed proceed on the assumption that contradictions really exist, by which their representatives find themselves called into question personally, politically, and professionally in their day and age, but this only further piques their eagerness for ever more contradictions. Hans Albert, for instance, says with reference to Karl R. Popper in a section of his 1968 *Treatise on Critical Reason* titled "Dialectical Thinking: The Search for Contradictions": "Search constantly for relevant contradictions in order to expose present convictions to the risk of refutation, so that they will have a chance to prove themselves."[9]

But Albert right away adds: "This quest is not recommended because contradictions are desired in themselves and must be preserved; nor, indeed, because one can thereby better take into account the contradictory nature of reality; but simply because when relevant contradictions emerge one has occasion, in accordance with the principle of noncontradiction, to revise one's convictions."[10]

The "contradictory nature of reality" has thus already been accepted here, meaning that "the search for contradictions" is axiomatic. The contradictions, however, no matter how "relevant," are nonetheless not desirable and should nonetheless not be perpetuated. Not their freedom, but the "principle of noncontradiction" is the authoritative watchword. Popper and Albert again show themselves to be successors of Aristotelian logic, which attempts to liberate from contradiction instead of liberating to it. Albert's contention that one should search, on the grounds of the principle of noncontradiction, for an occasion to "revise one's convictions," means merely this: one's own convictions, which have come up against contradictions, should—thanks to the challenge of the contradiction—be revised so as to no longer be subject to the challenge of the contradiction. For noncontradiction, as Popper puts it in his *The Logic of Scientific Discovery*, assumes a special position given the conditions that must be met by a theoretical system (system of axioms). "It can be regarded as the first of the requirements to be satisfied by *every* theoretical system, be it empirical or non-empirical."[11]

Endeavoring to completely eradicate contradiction in this way does not eradicate it, however, but merely dissipates it: now one is oneself in flight from it, without any possibility of escaping—as Albert himself must concede—the "contradictory nature" of its reality on the grounds of modernity.[12] Disciplinary idiots flee into the narrowness of their nonbindingly noncontradictory discipline just like futurologists flee into the no less nonbinding breadth of their science of the future. But the point is not to flee, but to hold one's ground!

To neither now nor in the future adhere to the conviction that, with each challenge and contradiction encountered, ultimate limits are drawn, but instead to go on trying to "revise" the conviction that has been called to account until the contradiction which challenges it has been eradicated, as if eradication of contradiction could ever again be possible: this strategy may nonetheless make one a great scientist. But it certainly and unfortunately also makes one a disciplinary idiot, that is to say, irresponsible in the worst and most culpable sense: guilty of attempting to dissipate contradiction.

Attempted annihilation

Reminded of their limits by the "contradictory nature" of modernity, many do not immediately perceive the progress it initiates. Namely that from now on, the challenge of every calling-to-account one musters will far outstrip, by virtue of this radically new quality of maturity, all merely quantitative growth. All they see, at least at first, is what has departed. They pit the "No" spoken in rejection of contradiction's past exclusion against the obsolete past of noncontradiction, instead of pitting noncontradiction's closure against the openness of the present and the future: the openness that has taken the place of that closure as a worthy, creative "Yes" inspired by a much greater degree of freedom.

But one hears and understands only this: that what had, but a moment before, been the truth, and was assumed to be the only truth, no longer holds. While it is true that, no matter had been held up as the truth, this single truth had never, as one well knows, been alone, and was thus only ever the panicked truth; whereas on the other hand, as one knows, every essential truth remains true along with every other essential truth. Nonetheless, and discerning above all the nullity of one's own truth's claim to singularity—and that of every other such truth, which had indeed been the truth in its respective "Middle Kingdom"—the hunger for faith and the thirst for knowledge, informed as they are by the past and the past of the past, land in the "dead-end-street of nihilism."[13]

And so once again a truth is taken to be the truth as such. If behind everything there is only nothing, then it would seem that this Nothing is everything; thanks to the power of the keys granted by its being worth literally nothing, there is once again a one-and-only truth!

Others have already built upon the dialectic. They dared take the step from the old insularities to the diversity of contradiction contained in the modern whole. But to their dismay, bitter disappointment, and boundless desperation, at the height of their dialectic, its proudly touted acknowledgment of the union of thesis and antithesis fails to set contradiction free.

Once again, a truth turns out to be nothing. And equally nothing are the theses and antitheses that the dialectic, if it does not annihilate them, at any rate invalidates from the perspective of its vision of the final synthesis. There is no return to what preceded the outcome of this dialectic; all that seems to remain is an All propelled towards the Nothing by its destroyers and defenders alike, everywhere and at all times at the mercy of deceit and irresponsibility.

To be sure, the Nothing is not conceded as such. Totalitarian and fascist oppression, the manipulative sabotaging of contradiction set free, and the futurological postponement and disciplinary-idiotic dissipation of the diversity of contradiction they acknowledge but do not sustain, fail—from the perspective of nihilism—to give the Nothing, which they too ultimately serve, the honor it deserves. Like the dialectic, which they themselves sometimes affirm and other times merely utilize, they all speak of maturity and of freedom and of a fundamentally new future, whereas what is behind all these slogans and their advocates is only the Nothing, which—according to nihilism—acts everywhere as co-regent and is the actual ruler of the All.

It matters little whether this Nothing of dawning annihilation and of the nullity and worthlessness of everything that exists shows its face often or just once: it is ultimately presumed to be everywhere. This insight leads once more to a singular belief and knowledge, a thoroughly unique saving grace. Nihilism is erupting, a "European nihilism," according to the trenchant heading of the first book of Nietzsche's *Will to Power*, written between 1884 and 1888. For nihilism emerged, as its mission and expansion show, from that whole that today encompasses the entire globe, which the antiquity and Middle Ages of the occidental world constructed with and against one another over three or four millennia. This is the nihilism about which Nietzsche thought he could predict that it would determine the history of the following two centuries. "I describe what is coming, what can no longer come differently: the advent of nihilism. This history can be related even now; for necessity itself is at work here."[14]

Yet no matter how sincere, and apparently very courageous, the negation of all phoniness may be, nihilism cannot extract itself from its own swamp, a no less untruthful arrogation of the truth: the "ism" of the Nothing itself. The root cause of being worth nothing, for which it attacks all previous confessions and knowledges and value judgments, remains its own reason for existence. It is preferable to reduce everything to Nothing than to finally, permanently, and boldly give up seeing everything as dependent upon a single truth taken to be the only truth. Nihilism thus always constitutes a dead-end street, but it is nonetheless a dead-end street that really exists.

Here I may recall my own Zurich dissertation of 1941, *Nihilism in the Light of a Critical Philosophy*.[15] It asked what nihilism is and answered: thanks to the faith and knowledge that all confessions, sciences, and values have nothing backing them up, it is the will to reduce all faith, knowledge, and value to this Nothing. The faith and knowledge of the Nothing behind everything constitute the *nihilistic premise*, the foundation, within a worthless All, of a new final faith and knowledge that joins forces with the will, the *nihilistic conclusion*, for the sake of a new final volition on the grounds of worthlessness. From the premise that "everything is nothing," faith and knowledge conclude that the Nothing is everything, and the will argues: "Therefore let everything be destroyed!"

The consequence of the contemplation of "futility" and of the faith that everything is worthy of perishing is, according to Nietzsche, that one lend a hand to its destruction. "This is, if you will, illogical; but the nihilist does not believe that one needs to be logical.—[...] The reduction to nothing by judgment"—this faith and knowledge of the Nothing at the back of everything—"is seconded by the reduction to nothing by hand":[16] the will to reduce everything to this Nothing. It may be desperation, but it may also be hope that seduces one into accepting this nihilistic conclusion, which deludes itself into imagining that when everything has been destroyed, there will be space for a new, once again fruitful existence. Even though nihilists destroy everything because everything seems to them null and void, their hope is that something new will thereby arise, just as Nietzsche himself clung to this hope.

> Actually, every major growth is accompanied by a tremendous crumbling and passing away: suffering, the symptoms of decline *belong* in the times of tremendous advances; every fruitful and powerful movement of humanity has also created at the same time a nihilistic movement. It could be the sign of a crucial and most essential growth, of the transition to new conditions of existence, that the most extreme form of pessimism, genuine *nihilism*, would come into the world. *This I have comprehended.*[17]

A distinction is thus to be made, in this we can agree with Nietzsche completely, who is only wrong to the extent that he ascribes a constructive meaning and even a creative force to some of nihilism's modes of expression, between provisional nihilism, on the one hand, and the active and passive expressive modes of permanent nihilism on the other. Provisional nihilism, of which Nietzsche says "we live in the midst of it,"[18] is at work wherever the rise of nihilism has already been conceded in a few focal points but is still being denied in others, as if something complete could be partially affirmed and partially denied. Yet this provisional nihilism has no other outcome than permanent nihilism, to which it is subject from the beginning, even before the conclusion of its provisional phases makes its permanence a certainty. At best, permanent nihilism gives rise to an impression of strength at the height of its active mode of expression, to the extent one can speak of strength at all with regard to nihilism.

Yet no matter how energetically or even joyfully productive the active mode of nihilism may commit itself to the work of "an*nihil*ation," in front of and behind it there is nonetheless only the Nothing, regardless of whether it acts full of hope and with deep satisfaction or without receiving any gratification of its own, even to its own torment. It may proceed with caution in one instance and too hastily in another, sometimes wallowing in cruelty, at others taking great pains to avoid it, nearly a friend of mankind, often a friend of animals, a friend of flowers; yet destruction alone follows upon it and characterizes it. Not for a single moment and in no way does the life nihilism tries to destroy—should it nonetheless persist or even blossom anew—flourish thanks to nihilism, for it is invariably unfruitful, everywhere barren.

Passive nihilism, by comparison, also goes beyond the nihilistic premise, but it either no longer can or no longer wants to put into practice the nihilistic conclusion of the will to Nothing but instead merely welcomes it. Everything seems void, from art and science and morality to politics, the economy, religion and philosophy, and therefore everything is worthy of perishing. Such passive nihilists are, however, much too disappointed, tired, or disgusted to actively push forward a destruction that is anyway also worthless in itself. Without purposefully intervening in existence, they live out their lives as inertly as possible. Correctly or not, Nietzsche identifies Buddhism as the most famous manifestation of passive nihilism, for which "whatever refreshes, heals, calms, numbs emerges into the foreground in various disguises, religious or moral, or political, or aesthetic"[19] and remains nothing but disguise, and the disguise of one and the same: Nothing.

If the outcome of provisional nihilism is permanent nihilism, the outcome of actively or passively permanent nihilism is the always increasingly desperate dead end of an*nihil*ation. No matter how effectively nihilists may derive strength and power from the other whose life they threaten, and from the conditions under which they take their other's life, such living strength and fruitful power as issues from their victims they can catch the light of only ever fleetingly. On their own they are incapable even of maintaining strength, power, fortitude, or essential meaning, let alone of calling them into existence anew.

To be sure, the contradiction that begins to announce itself through nihilistic an*nihil*ation cannot be taken seriously enough by those whom it calls into question. But no matter how often nihilism may be in the right, it does not offer its own direction to those it conveys into the void. That is why it is, as the comparison with anarchism will soon make clear, thoroughly unproductive, in contrast to the counter-productivity of anarchism. Nihilism is just the repetition of what is null and worthless in every direction, only with the addition that this time, one is conscious of the worthlessness. But—and in opposition to anarchism, which clearly perceives what is right but fails to realize it in a way that can bear fruit—nihilism is and remains, even after it has spoken its truth, incapable of even perceiving the truths whose trajectories lead not to the Nothing, but further: beyond the Nothing and beyond every nihilism!

Chapter 7

THE CHALLENGE OF CONTRADICTION

Outraged freedom

Outrage over what is outraging in the world is the motivating factor behind the contradiction represented by anarchism. And because what goes on in the world is indeed outraging, anarchism is not merely a passing phase of contrariness, like childhood defiance or puberty—given one condition. Its contradiction must rise up in the name of freedom. Only when freedom—and it alone—constitutes the driving force and the decisive goal of outraged insurrection, are we speaking of anarchism. And so although anarchism, for which nothing but freedom is of any consequence, is always to be challenged on account of its exaggerated one-sidedness, it nonetheless remains an authentic intellectual movement. The freedom that constitutes its core concern is not in question as such.

What should be questioned, however, is the absoluteness of insisting not only that everything should become free, but that freedom itself should be everything: freedom freely for freedom's sake, freedom always, freedom everywhere.

Nihilism is different. "The Nothing is everything, and everything should become nothing!" How stark a contrast to the slogan of anarchism, which says freedom is everything and everything should become free! This is why nihilism constitutes a dead end even when it is right, whereas anarchism is never a dead end, even when it is wrong. So while nihilism must be overcome, anarchism must be surpassed! If nihilism is deprived of the foundation of its appeal to the Nothing, the path that no longer leads to nothing arrives here, where it parts ways with nihilism. Anarchism, however, whose aim—freedom—is by no means nothing, can only be surpassed along its own trajectory; this requires striking out on the path of anarchism while leaving behind both the outrageousness by which anarchism is provoked and the provocative absoluteness with which it induces outrage.

But what about the violence of anarchism? Aren't anarchists men who hurl bombs and consciously and methodically dedicate their lives to crime? In view of this objection, the following differentiation must be kept in mind.

For as long as anarchists have committed themselves to violence, which neither Godwin, Proudhon, or Stirner, the originators of anarchism, did, but which was only first propagated by Bakunin, there have also been anarchists who have committed themselves to nonviolence, as Tolstoy did the moment Bakunin called for "direct action." Declare yourselves free from violence, from all violence, Tolstoy called out to the workers,[1] heralding the "great refusal" many decades before Marcuse, who would merely lend it a new explosive power. Marcuse teaches nonviolence as the most effective expression of the outrage not of workers, but of socially marginalized groups. And Tolstoy had already said, in an attempt to dissuade the workers from using the weapon of violence Marxism indicated:

> In trying to oppose violence to violence, you workingmen do what a man bound with ropes would do if, to free himself, he should tug at the ropes: he only tightens the knots that fetter him. The same is true as regards your attempts by means of violence to take away what is withheld from you by means of violence.[2]

Nonetheless, anarchism too has succumbed to the temptation of violence, which, it should be said, has dishonored every great movement of humanity, mocking the message of love in one instance, the message of peace in another, and in anarchism's case, the message of freedom. But the notion that anarchism has been more prone to violence than any other movement is nothing but a myth in the negative sense of the word, a defamation propagated by its enemies.

Precisely because every anarchism ultimately rises up in outrage against violence—regardless of whether it pursues its demand for freedom with violence, following Bakunin, or without it, following Tolstoy—the violence its outrage must invariably confront is always represented in relation to that outrage as if the outrage were not a denunciation of violence, but itself worthy of denunciation as violence. With perfidious swiftness, anarchism has become the scapegoat of the great majority of those whom it calls into question, those who not only really do make use of violence, but who are also capable of exploiting their power in order to shift the responsibility for it to their victims. Finally, what began as a consciously contrived "projection" is further elaborated unconsciously until even the victims themselves begin to believe they are guilty of the violence that has been displaced onto them, although they are the least guilty of all.

The least guilty! For it is to anarchism and to its freedom, which springs from outrage—rather than to Gandhi for example, for whom Tolstoy paved the way—that we owe the creation of the doctrine of nonviolence and the perennial renewal and resurgence of its exhortation.

The bomb-toting anarchist has always been there, especially since the invention of dynamite in 1867 unleashed waves of excitement about the explosive power of bombs, a cutting-edge technological revolution that was, thanks to its "progressiveness," a particularly enticing temptation. On the other hand, the use of bombs and the employment of much more murderous weapons by both the political right and the political left has also always been a reality, just as it—according to Tolstoy—always is and always will be the reality wherever states exist. They may enshrine the violence by which they exercise their power in law or, as they are entitled to do by so-called "right," they may elevate their own violence above that law, even while they continue to subject their citizens to it with merciless severity. In either case, it is for both freedom and the citizenry literally life itself which is at stake. The—from a legal point of view—thoroughly irreproachable execution that Count Tolstoy simply could not miss on the early Paris morning of April 6, 1857, was thus an experience from which he emerged a permanently outraged rebel, an enemy of every future use of violence without exception.

> A stout white neck and chest; he kissed the Gospels, and then—death. How senseless! ... The guillotine kept me long awake, and compelled me to reflect. What is certain is that henceforward I shall never serve any government. All governments in this world are equal in the measure of good and evil that they do. The only ideal is anarchy.[3]

Freedom contra the state

Has anarchism always existed, simply because what goes on in the world has always been outraging? Is Tolstoy's "Ideal of Anarchy" the expression of every rebellion provoked by this outrage? Was, then, the destruction of images in the "Iconoclasm" of the Jewish "Exodus" from Egypt already anarchism? And the Hijra of Mohammed's migration from Mecca and Luther's "Protestantism," were they already anarchism, just like—for Proudhon and Tolstoy—primitive Christianity was: the forging of a path to the "freedom of the glory of the children of God" (Rom. 8:21)?

The answer is an unambiguous "No." If we are to establish clearly what anarchism means for modernity, we must not confuse what it essentially is: outraged rebellion provoked by the specific situation of modernity, provocatively challenging this modernity in its specificity.

Whenever iconoclasm has arisen in the past, such as that which, provoked by the surprisingly successful abolishment of the image in the Arab world, nearly destroyed Roman Byzantium—and this already indicates the decisive difference—at its core was a clearly defined purpose set on avoiding a specific form of idolatry, and it rose up against this idolatry on the basis of the biblical commandment against graven images: "You shall not make for yourself a sculptured image, any likeness of what is in the heavens above, or on the earth below, or in the waters below the earth" (Exod. 20:4; Deut. 5:8). Even where iconoclasm remained in its state of outrage, or at least in the gesture of outrage, its contradiction was directed against an ambition it intended to replace with its own. And having established this new foundation—or at least initiated its establishment in an apparently unstoppable way—one could rest content, having finally risen to power oneself.

But anarchism is not the kind of upheaval that conspires against the power that outrages it, and against which it rebels, merely so it can rise to power itself; it is, rather, outrage and insurrection as such, and that means revolt rather than revolution. *Le Révolté* was, appropriately, the title of the magazine Kropotkin founded in 1876, the year of Bakunin's death. It is a foundational work of anarchism: conscious of itself as outrage in the sense of revolt, which neither his important predecessor nor Proudhon had succeeded in distinguishing so clearly from the revolutions that only ever aim at regime change, instead of building all power without exception—including one's own—on the foundation of freedom.

Nothing is more meaningless than the question that is put to anarchism over and over again, the question of its goal. And nothing is more ridiculous than the pretense—often boastful of its own ostensible permissiveness—of a willingness to engage with anarchism and perhaps even to accept it, if only it would specify its goal. Precisely this would divest anarchism of its motive force, for it is directed against every movement that has put itself in the service of a purpose, because any purpose would only provoke new outrage. Anarchism really doesn't have a goal. It must first of all be acknowledged that this is its own interpretation of freedom, which substantiates its reality. This is the root of anarchism's exhilarating audacity, and this is also the root—as will be demonstrated here for the first time—of the dangers such a buoyantly anarchist interpretation of freedom entails and of the counterproductive effects to which it can give rise.

On the other hand, anarchism is not alone. The Impressionist movement in painting, as well as photography and sociology emerged at the same time, further substantiating it as a rebellion characteristic of modernity, the particular form of an outrage that takes modernity to task according to its and only its particular challenges. Alongside other "contemporaries" of the revolt against the "establishment" of church and state, or against the "status" as Stirner called it, meaning the dominant "tissue and plexus of dependence and adherence,"[4] anarchism puts its trust in the "spontaneity" of its own immediacy, which thus far only "chance"—to use one of anarchism's favorite words—has prevented from establishing the new world.

In this vein, Proudhon's countryman, friend, and confederate Courbet moved out of his studio, as droves of painters after him would move out of their studios and free themselves from their dependence on commissioners, thus becoming the first Impressionists in the proper sense, with the self-conscious anarchist Pissarro leading the way. By opening themselves up to the "impression" of the nearest, most contingent details of nature, the *impression* of the world was to be vindicated in the here and now, and by the splendor of their art, they would offer irrefutable testimony that merely being open can indeed be enough.

At the same time, photographers were seeking, in literally every blink of the eye—which it had never been possible, prior to the nineteenth century, to eternalize so "impartially"—to bring the truth of the world to present awareness. The "chance" invention of photography could now also bear witness to the thousandfold right and unalienable truth of every feeling without exception, even the most "fleeting," no matter how or where it stirred.

And sociologists dared avert their gaze from the prescribed orders of the world of states, and to entrust themselves instead to the human world, to the uncertain origins and pathways of its flows. No matter how long the law of the state maintains its significance, no matter how long the state's violent exercise of domination continues—this order—only ever a top-down arrangement—leaves, in the eyes of the sociologists, what is actual, that which alone embodies the reality of life, unaccounted for: society. Even before states existed and as long as they shall, and even when they once again no longer exist, there is and will be, running athwart of each of their configurations, society: communal life as such, in some form or another.

"For freedom to exist, freedom must be free,"[5] Proudhon declared after the collapse of the 1848 Revolution, recapitulating his experiences while imprisoned at Saint-Pélagie and at times reflecting on his own participation in the political violence.

> Invent, speculate, ponder as much as you want, just don't force your ideas upon the people. Freedom, freedom always and freedom alone and no governmentalism! This is the entire revolutionary catechism.[6] [...] Instead of trying to seize the authority of the state, just ask it to stop meddling in everything. And teach the people to secure their own prosperity and order without state assistance.[7] [...] No more domination of human beings by other human beings through the amassing of force! No more exploitation of the human being by the power of accumulating money! Freedom! This is the first and last word of every social philosophy.[8]

Speaking of anarchism thus requires appreciating it in relation to its adversary, the aforementioned hegemonic "tissue and plexus of dependence and adherence."[9] In both manifestations—initially as the immediate exercise of power, which bestows authority all down the line, from the king "down to the beadle,"[10] and as the rapidly expanding, increasingly indirect rule of bureaucratic administration—it is the modern state that has provoked the outrage of anarchism and will continue to provoke ever new manifestations of anarchism by providing occasion upon occasion for renewed outrage and revolt. "Is not self-will being lost while we attend to the will for order?"[11] Stirner asked early on, foreseeing and preemptively pillorying the future power of the "party," this "state within the state."[12] The party, too, represents the "idea of order," which ignores the "self-will" of every individual's personal meaning. And so the individual—each and every one "unique"—is deprived of his or her selfhood, deprived literally of what is his or her "own," the very reason all human beings and all individuals want to, ought to, and can be themselves: that is to say, free!

> Our societies and States *are* without our *making* them [...][13] Thus the independent establishment of the State founds my lack of independence, its condition as a "natural growth," its organism, demands that my nature not grow freely, but be cut to fit it.[14] [...] In the State the *party* is current. [...] One hears nothing oftener now than the admonition to remain true to his party [...] In short, the party cannot bear non-partisanship [...] What matters the party to me? I shall find enough anyhow who *unite* with me without swearing allegiance to my flag.[15]

With the exception of Godwin, a forerunner of anarchism who failed to make headway in his native England—and whose *Enquiry Concerning Political Justice and Its Influence on Morals and Happiness* had, in 1793, not yet made history—the heyday of anarchism falls between 1840 and 1882. Proudhon's *What Is Property?* and Stirner's *The Ego and His Own* mark the threshold years of 1840 and 1844, while Bakunin's, Kropotkin's, and Tolstoy's adoptions of anarchism in the years 1862, 1876, and 1882 mark its conclusion.

It was at that time the state, the "power state" [*Machtstaat*] in Germany, France, and Russia, such as it had never before existed, that within a single decade outraged the young Stirner, Proudhon, and Bakunin, born in 1806, 1809, and 1814, respectively. This state was, as the European reaction to the French Revolution and the Napoleonic counterrevolution, now the state of universal military conscription, compulsory education, and taxation as well as—in order to better wage war domestically and abroad—a state that not only funded, but also oversaw scientific research and with increasing recklessness commandeered and applied technology until it ultimately took over every aspect of training, provision, and healthcare, which up to that point had belonged to the sphere of each individual's responsibility for the conduct of his or her life and had constituted the freedom and dignity of conscience.

"Always the state! Herr Papa! As the church was proclaimed and looked upon as the 'mother' of believers, so the State has altogether the face of the provident father,"[16] Stirner bemoans and rants and mocks. But on the other hand, this state is also but a "historical, transitory institution," as Bakunin's posthumous 1871 work *God and the State* teaches.[17] At that time, although the Paris Commune had already been quashed, it had nonetheless also been realized. "A temporary form of society,"[18] that is what the state is:

> like its elder brother the Church. [...] Man has been born into society [...] Society precedes the human individual and at the same time it survives him, like nature itself [...] So there is just as little point in asking whether society is good or evil [...] The state is another matter, and I have no hesitation in saying that the State is evil, but an historically necessary evil, as necessary in the past as its utter extinction will eventually become in the future [...] The State is authority, force on display, infatuation with power [...] So even while commanding the good it frustrates and despoils it, precisely because it does command [...] The liberty, morality and human dignity of man consists in his doing good not because he is compelled but because he conceives, desires and loves it.[19]

In this way, two mutually exclusive ultimate truths collide, each with the weight of an entire reality that calls its adversary, who is also present, irreconcilably into question. The state and the freedom of the citizen contradict one another to the point of conflict, a collision they can as such only ever escalate in increasingly stark opposition to one another. The state, because its power also posits the law, will brand freedom's power unjust, such that freedom, outrage, destruction, and violence appear to be one and the same! Nonetheless, the struggle here is not merely between order and disorder; rather, it is a struggle between two different conceptions of "self-will" [*Eigensinn*] and their respective conceptions of justice.

7. The Challenge of Contradiction

The anarchists unfurling their black banners are the successors of the peasant revolts and hunger riots of the late medieval and early modern periods, whose overpowering outrage and momentum lives on in them. And when the call for the Commune, this "community" rings out, the demand is for nothing other than the ancient communal freedom that existed before the state, which took it away without offering anything better. The councils, or "Soviets," only recall the successful self-management of once flourishing communities whose freedom was finally quashed by the modern state as if they had been breeding grounds of enraging disorder. Whereby the state for its own part ushered in no less disorder than the councils were ever guilty of unleashing but only managed to provoke their longing for freedom anew. And in this way, the federalist exercise of power "from the bottom up," in which Proudhon rehabilitated something old, but not obsolete—the mutual safeguarding of freedoms among united cooperatives [*Bundesgenossenschaften*]—contradicts every hierarchical exercise of power "from the top down" and is nonetheless, or for this very reason, not merely an advocate of disorder vis-à-vis the claim to represent order and nothing but order.

If neither of these adversaries outraged the other, the outrage of the other truth that is thereby challenged would never arise; but arise it does, and for the sake of what it has witnessed differently, this truth now also takes up the challenge: as anarchism—of provocation.

Freedom through challenge

Thus far the world has seen four major anarchist challenges, each occasioned by a challenge to anarchism's demand for freedom, that "self-will" which has already been pronounced dead twice, most prominently in 1938.

The classical years of anarchism began with Proudhon and Stirner and ended with Tolstoy, with social anarchism emerging from France, individualist anarchism arising in Germany, and the Russians Bakunin and Tolstoy providing versions of anarchism allied either with violence or, on the contrary, committed to nonviolence. But between 1882 and 1905, after the failure of the Paris Commune and the introduction of parliamentary participation (or at least the pretense of it), the loss, first with bloodshed and then without it, of the most energetic and active anarchists, led to a kind of stasis. Anarchism was pronounced dead even while it was still being vilified as a terrifying boogeyman. For anarchism was none the less still afoot, providing the state—even as it jubilantly celebrated anarchism's demise—with a not unwelcome justification for permanent militarization. This meant that whenever the challenge to the state—represented by anarchism—failed to materialize, the state might even provoke it itself. This was a period of progress for the theory of anarchism, above all in the works of Kropotkin, Tolstoy, Landauer, and Mackay, who rediscovered Stirner; whereas the "praxis" that emerged alongside it, consisting of individual actions and impatient acts of violence, failed to bring about empowerment but instead consistently reinforced the power of the state. Nonetheless, the state's celebration of its triumph was premature.

Between 1905 and 1938, the revolution's repeated victories from Russia to Spain also created opportunities for anarchism to put itself to the test. Each of these tests ended prematurely, but only on account of the subterfuge and overwhelming force of its enemies, and only after it had already been demonstrated that anarchism was indeed a fruitful possible form of communal life. Once the state authority has been toppled and the revolution itself has not yet become the state authority, governance must begin at the bottom and move upward granting such an extensive priority to freedom as no state, given its essence, can bear, and which the revolution tolerates only with reluctance. If people could be productive together, in freedom and on the basis of freedom, then the revolution that had succeeded in toppling the regime would no longer need to come to power—which is, however, and contrary to anarchism—ultimately its only concern. The Russian Spring of 1905 and the Russian Winter of 1917/18 forced anarchism to prove itself. Later, it proved itself again in Makhno's Ukraine and finally—this time over a course of years—in republican Spain, whose anarchism went back to Bakunin himself and the survivors of the Paris Commune. This was one more attempt to realize the same project of which Kropotkin has left an unforgettable account:

> "I shall always remember," a friend told us, "those beautiful moments of deliverance. I went down from my attic room on the Latin quarter to join in that immense open air club which filled the boulevards from one end of Paris to the other. [...] Even the bourgeoisie, carried away by the universal ardour, looked on joyfully as the new world unfolded itself. If it is necessary to carry out the social revolution—very well, let's do it; let us put everything in common; we are ready for that!" The elements of the revolution were in place; it was only necessary to put them into operation. Going back to my room that evening, I said to myself: "How wonderful humanity is! I always condemned it in the past because I never understood it!"[20]

Yet on the other hand, the Paris Commune, like the particularly deep-rooted and long-flourishing anarchism of Spain, did in the end fail. "[T]he defeat of that movement in 1937 [...] marked the end of anarchism as a serious political force, even if it still survives as an intellectual one," James Joll wrote twenty-seven years later in *The Anarchists*.[21] But towards the end of that same year, 1964, anarchism suddenly reappeared on the scene, this time also as a political force. Two mutually independent processes initiated the fourth epoch of anarchism. The first of these were the student revolts in Berkeley and Berlin, which forced anarchism to be taken seriously. The other was that which provided them with their slogans, Marcuse's book *The One-dimensional Man*. No matter how often its demise is declared, the end of anarchism is still not in view.

It is of no consequence that both of these breakthroughs initially tried to conceive of themselves as reforms of Marxism, and thus as the "New Left," instead of as anarchism in the sense opposed by the tradition stretching from Marx to

Lenin! Marx and Lenin are only on the margins here, whereas in essence it is the spirit of Proudhon, Stirner, Bakunin, Tolstoy, and Kropotkin that was revived.

A question for itself in this regard concerns the immediate occasion for this new revolt. To be sure, the necessity of defending the world against those who had unleashed the Second World War in 1939 pushed everything else outraging about the world into the background, even if it went on being the same outraging world it was before. Rescuing the world itself was the top priority, just as after the war's victorious conclusion, the task of rebuilding it succeeded once again in repressing everything else. Then, however, it began to come to light, and with every passing day it was ever more difficult to ignore. The world that was being rebuilt was turning out to be just as outraging, if not more prone to provoking outrage, than ever before. This was not a new world; the old world had risen again: an ever-expanding state constantly increasing its power, violence, and bureaucracy from above was constraining human freedom to an unprecedented degree. And then, when the good Pope John died on June 3, 1963, and President Kennedy was murdered on November 22, 1963, it seemed—outrageously—that every hope of any of the world's outrageous injustices ever being changed from the top down had to be buried with them.

But the world can and will be transformed fundamentally from the bottom up, Marcuse teaches, asking two questions in a new way and answering them better than they had been answered by Marx and his successors. In doing so, he likewise positions himself as a successor of Marx, despite his adherence to psychoanalysis. The legacy of Marx can be combined with that of Freud!

Who in the world can transform outrage about the world into an act of radical historical intervention, and how can it be done? These are Marcuse's questions, and he answers them like this: none other than the outsiders, ostracized in and by the world, whom even the most prosperous "affluent society" passes over with disdain. The old, the young, the ill, the unemployed and those branded "unemployed," the students barred from all meaningful participation in decision-making, the countless minorities as well as the globally neglected masses of peoples in the developing nations—these are the people who can and will fundamentally transform their outraging world. For in the course of the late nineteenth and early twentieth centuries, the proletariat of Marxism—which had once been the particularly ruthlessly exploited fourth estate of a society that served the church, the nobility, and the bourgeoisie—became that establishment's "conservative popular base."[22] Assuming it ever was in a position to transform the world (as whose "popular base" it subsisted) from the bottom up, it is now either no longer in that position or at least no longer willing.

The path to fundamentally changing the world is indeed open, not for the proletariat, but for these outsiders in whose ostracization the proletariat also joins in, and it is a path that cannot be blocked. It opens up as soon as the insurgents begin to harness the force of their powerlessness. It is upon this challenge, the "provocation" of Marcuse's "Great Refusal" that they ought to build! This is, after answering the question of the agent of global change, the answer Marcuse gives to the second question of how it can be brought about. "When they get together and go into the streets, without arms, without protection, in order to ask for the most primitive civil rights, they know that they face dogs, stones, and bombs, jail, concentration camps, even death [...] [T]he fact that they start refusing to play the game may be the fact which marks the beginning of the end of a period."[23]

The Communist Manifesto of 1848 had still derided these ostracized outsiders of the world as the "Lumpenproletariat," signifying the "passively rotting mass thrown off by the lowest layers of old society";[24] but only twenty-five years later, Bakunin already understood clearly the significance these bottom-most levels held for cataclysmic, global change. As the dregs of every "new society" towards which the workforce strives, they are the true nucleus of all future activity. It is not they who are rotting, but society—including its workforce—looking down on them in their "decay." "What predominates in Italy is that destitute proletariat to which Marx and Engels, and, following them, the whole school of German social democrats, refer with the utmost contempt. They do so completely in vain, because here, and here alone, not in the bourgeois stratum of workers, is to be found the mind as well as the might of the future social revolution."[25]

And this spirit and this strength were indeed present, and repeatedly made their historical impact felt, as soon as that *Lumpenproletariat* that Marx and Engels had mocked, and which Bakunin extolled, and which Marcuse called the "outcasts and outsiders"[26]—as soon as they had grasped, as Tolstoy's yet unacknowledged successors, that defiance is the lever with which the outraging world can be unhinged. Just as Bakunin surpassed Marx, Tolstoy in this regard surpassed Bakunin. Where every other means of changing the world fails—because, despite being a powerful weapon, it is either defeated by an even more powerful weapon or because, after an initial victory, it succumbs to the same abuse of power against which the outraged first stood up in revolt—defiance succeeds because it does not attempt to do more than expose every form of power, and every weapon, as enemies of freedom. If the powers that be defend themselves against the provocation, then there can be no doubt that they are enemies of freedom. But if they do not defend themselves, then they are its enemies all the more. In the first case they bar the path to freedom with violence, provoking general outrage, and in the second case—if and because they don't defend themselves—they bar the path to freedom in a way that makes an impression of mere arrogance, giving rise to almost greater outrage.

If the demand for freedom contents itself with defying that world in which what passes for normalcy is an outrage, and if it provokes the world's outrageousness to ever more outraging spectacles, the powerlessness of the demand for freedom can, or could, really change the world—if the people who share this demand got together, in spite of their powerlessness, and went out into the streets, without weapons and without protection—were it not for this: even freedom itself, in whose name the thirst for freedom stands up in revolt, is an enemy of freedom or can at any rate become one. The degree of freedom that anarchism was the first to secure is too often lost again when the freedom already realized by anarchism turns against the very freedom it is trying to realize.

7. The Challenge of Contradiction

Freedom contra freedom

That freedom which, according to the watchword of anarchism, should be everything: freedom arising from freedom for the sake of freedom, and freedom everywhere and at all times, can, although it is never merely unproductive, act as a deterrent—which is to say, become counterproductive—when anarchism entrusts to freedom more than freedom alone can fulfill and entrusts to its own means of pursuing freedom more than it can deliver when put to the test. It is not only freedom that is needed, but contradiction set free. Everyone and everything else must also have its say, not only each person him- or herself.

But only those who take freedom—in the sense of contradiction set free—even more seriously than anarchism does have the right to confront it with the reproach that it does not—yet—take freedom as seriously as it requires to be taken. As a voice of conscience, anarchism refuses to let us forget how outraging every violation of freedom is. But only a more successful realization of freedom, and that alone—which, instead of forbidding anarchism from pursuing its course, would have to surpass it along its own trajectory—can, in good conscience, remind anarchism that it too falls short of freedom, despite the fact that its will to be the fulfillment of freedom constitutes the essence of its greatness and the basis of its renown.

Chapter 8

THE CONTRADICTIONS OF FREEDOM

Freedom instead of subjugation

The decampment to freedom is a threefold event. It is set in motion by two steps taken by Greco-Roman antiquity, and one step taken by Jewish antiquity.

The path of freedom begins with freedom in the external sense. This is the freedom individuals or states enjoy from subjugation by another without calling subjugation as such into question. From here, the path leads to freedom as the ownership of one's own essence, as something impervious to any external influence. Once this internalized freedom liberates itself from all external influence, it can even be condemned once more to external subjugation without thereby forfeiting its inner freedom. Like freedom in the outward sense, freedom in the inward sense acquiesces in subjugation from which it knows itself to be free: in its own world, independent of the world beyond.

Yet freedom, as experienced and taught by Judaism, is both outwardly and inwardly a measure of the historical development of every person and of all peoples without exception, and its goal is their freedom's complete realization. These two steps towards freedom, first of all towards outward freedom with its locally and individually limited scope and towards the spiritually universal freedom of inwardness, are joined by the step towards messianic freedom as freedom as such. "You shall proclaim liberty throughout the land for all its inhabitants" (Lev. 25:10) becomes a worldwide proclamation calling subjugation, and that is to say every form of subjugation without exception, fundamentally into question. That subjugation that in part still existed, and reappeared time and again, should not exist, and one day it no longer would exist!

And yet the Greco-Roman development of freedom was also magnificent and inspiring in taking its two unforgettable steps along the path towards the dignity and empowered maturity of the self.

During the fifth century BCE, classical Greece succeeded in making humanity conscious—first of all—of a fundamental difference between being free and unfree. And yet the fact that the flipside of one's own freedom was the unfreedom of the other did not present any quandary whatsoever; on the contrary, it was something to be proud of. So that several tens of thousands of individuals and a few city-states could be free, subjugation was to be the fate of all other people and states and remain so forever. The freedom of this step towards freedom is locally constrained and thoroughly egoistic—and although it constituted an important step forward toward politics, it was ultimately content to ensure its own freedom from subjugation.

Nonetheless, this is the root of the ever-misleading "myth of East versus West"[1] that persists even today, according to which one uses one's own freedom to debase one's other, instead of being inspired by the value of freedom to the shared nature of its calling. The fifth-century Greeks and their spokesperson Herodotus were of course in the right to extol their battle against the Persians as a defense of their freedom, but they were in the wrong as soon as they derived from it the ideology of a struggle of freedom versus servitude, as if their own West were in essence unwaveringly free, and the East in essence exclusively unfree, and in this regard unchangeable. Soon the West, having neglected the extent to which servitude existed in its own world, lost its freedom once again. For far too long, until and even after its freedom had been forfeited, the political subjugation that threatened Greece from Macedonia and Rome was not taken seriously. Blinded by the apparent immunity they had gloriously demonstrated at Marathon and Salamis, the Greeks believed themselves to be essentially superior to the East, characterized as it was by servitude.

But is someone who is, like the Greeks at the height of their classical period, free relative to the servitude of others really free? Shouldn't one try instead to be inwardly free, independent of everything external? Can't a person who is inwardly free, even one who is outwardly subject to servitude, be free and, ultimately, even more free than those who are merely outwardly free? This was what the Greeks were soon asking themselves, as later the Romans would, after they had once more lost a measure of the celebrated freedom of their western world, or could at least no longer be certain of it.

In an all too brief moment of insight in which he comprehends that slavery—an indispensable condition of the continued existence of his world—is merely a result of his world's technological underdevelopment, Aristotle says:

> For if each tool could perform its own task at our bidding or anticipating it, and if [...] shuttles shuttled to and fro of their own accord, and pluckers played lyres, then master-craftsmen would have no need of assistants nor masters any need of slaves.[2]

Yet the loom and the lyre do not—at least not yet—weave or play on their own. That is why there are masters and lords on the one hand, and assistants and slaves on the other, that is to say tools; and although they are "a superior tool among tools," "animate tools," they are ultimately only tools and nothing more.[3]

And yet, as Aristotle goes on to say, and in so doing paves the way for the second step in the decampment to freedom: neither the outward freedom of the master and the lord nor the revocation of this outward freedom, the reduction of human beings to "animate tools," which, like tools without souls, represent merely the personal chattels and property of their respective owners, divested of any will of their own—neither condition provides a guarantee that being a master or lord means one is truly free or that being an assistant or servant means one has truly lost one's freedom.

For that which is decreed by the laws of the world and of human beings is supplemented by what human beings are by nature. The children of free people can be slavish, while children born into and intended for servitude can have the souls of free men.[4] Nonetheless—and this is what Aristotle and the subsequent centuries of Greco-Roman antiquity, including Paul, settle for—subjugation exists and must exist, but from now on, only in the form of outward subjugation. A slave, Paul writes to the Corinthians, has no concern for his or her status and should prefer to remain a slave even if he or she could become free, for even as a slave he or she is in deed and truth God's "freed person" (Cor. 1, 7:20–22). Where freedom tips the balance, no slave is slavish simply because he or she is a slave: only what a person is in soul and spirit matters.

To be sure, this is already a better conception of freedom, for it is no longer merely an external possession, dependent on external conditions. And it is—conceived as the freedom of the soul of every person—a universal possession! What now comes into view is that all human beings without exception are called to freedom, despite all external differences between them. But this liberation to a global fellowship of inwardness leads into the cul-de-sac of another, further misunderstanding of freedom. In defiance of every form of dependence, the internalization of freedom seduced, and goes on seducing time and again, into apathy regarding one's own external conditions, even if they are conditions of dependence.

And so a further step is necessary to supplement the progress achieved through internalization, and this was accomplished by the biblical epoch of Jewry, which also developed internalization in its own right. This people was led out of the land of Egypt, the insistently pilloried "house of bondage," whereby it truly became the people it is for the first time: the people of the covenant, owing to the historic act of liberation (Exod. 20:2, Deut. 5:6). Freedom—as Jeremiah proclaimed when the leading class of his contemporaries refused to take seriously the mandate requiring them to free their servants and maids after no more than seven years—demands the abolishment of all slavery in as real and complete a way as the liberation from the Egyptian house of bondage truly and completely established the freedom of Israel (34:8 ff.). He furthermore combined this emancipation—a "letting run free" [*Freilauf*], as Buber puts it—with the stipulation that they not be let go "empty-handed." Whether servant or maid, "furnish him out of the flock, threshing-floor, and vat, with which the Lord your God has blessed you" (Deut. 15:14) at the beginning of the seventh year.

"If a fellow Hebrew, man or woman, is sold to you, he shall serve you six years, and in the seventh year you shall set him free" (Exod. 21:2; Deut. 15:12; Jer. 34:14).

It was on account of those who did not hesitate, as soon as the danger seemed to have been averted, to revoke the freedom that had finally been granted to their unfree compatriots under the most dire conditions of war, that Jeremiah proclaimed freedom in such a terrifyingly real and, with reference to "all the kingdoms of the earth," truly global sense: a freedom that would, by the same token, come to real and global fruition:

"You would not obey me and proclaim a release, each to his kinsman and countryman. Lo! I proclaim your release—declares the Lord—to the sword, to pestilence, and to famine; and I will make you a horror to all the kingdoms of the earth" (34:17).

Freedom despite liberation

What freedom is, this freedom that is understood at first only externally, then internalized, and finally—from within—demanded of the entire external world as complete freedom; what this freedom is cannot be understood within the framework of the old debate about free will. That debate only serves to divert attention from what freedom really is and from what its realization means.

For regardless of whether a will makes its own decisions or decisions that eventuate according to predetermination, one's responsibility for one's actions and their consequences remains the same. Determinists and indeterminists were always in agreement on this point, independently of the fanatically defended determinacy of the will advanced by the former and the no less fanatically propagated indeterminacy of the will of the latter. Human beings must, according to the views of both predestination and fatalism, answer for their actions in just the same way, as if it were they themselves who thereby proved themselves, or they themselves who failed in whatever it was that proved to be their failing, be it on account of their irrevocable predestination, as in the former case, or of their unavoidable destiny, as in the latter.

But there are two other tensions and several others more that place us directly into the center of the reality of freedom, which is not achieved by disarming every conceivable contradiction in a limitless expanse of "freedom from contradiction" but can only be reached along the narrow ridge that leads to the summit of freedom's contradictions. Is freedom the fancy-free boundlessness of fool's license? This question sets the first point of tension, the second of which presents the following consideration. Does liberation have to liberate to boundlessness if we also consider that the ultimate concern of freedom is commitments and that boundlessness opens the way not only to this path, but also to its detours and pitfalls, to countless temptations and seductions?

Is freedom the same thing as fool's license, caprice? This is the first question to be asked. Is caprice—the will to be free to do anything at all a will can wish, be it reasonable or senseless, feasible or unfeasible—freedom? Or is freedom only freedom when a will decides against the arbitrariness of its desires for only those possibilities that enable it to bear fruit in an individually and socially human sense? At stake here is the clear Either-Or of deciding between boundlessness on one side and commitment on the other. Is freedom the boundlessness of refusing every binding duty? Or is freedom the decision for commitments: the deliberate assumption of henceforth binding obligations?

8. The Contradictions of Freedom

The answer, unambiguous answer, can only be that freedom is not mere caprice, not this limitless arbitrariness of sometimes wanting and sometimes not wanting, according to a moment's whim. Quite apart from that, it nonetheless remains true that there is good reason for granting, at least once a year, free passage to the fool's license of the Saturnalia and Carnival and Purim. Wholly in vain, however, says Goethe, and rightly so:

Wholly in vain will uncommitted spirits
Strive upward towards accomplishment's pure peak.
Desiring greatness means self-limitation:
The master's he who pulls himself together,
And nothing but the law can set us free.

Vergebens werden ungebundne Geister
Nach der Vollendung reiner Höhe streben.
Wer Großes will, muß sich zusammenraffen;
In der Beschränkung zeigt sich erst der Meister,
Und das Gesetz nur kann uns Freiheit geben.[5]

There is, however, also another boundlessness, which is also not the freedom that it—like the boundlessness of caprice—would have us believe it is, but which must be hazarded nevertheless for the sake of freedom itself. Without real and literally unconditional freedom from commitment, freedom cannot decide in favor of the law within whose limits, as Goethe says, the master proves him- or herself as such. A person who desires greatness must pull him- or herself together! But the ability to pull oneself together also presupposes—if it is to be an act of freedom—its opposite, the possibility of scoffing at self-possession and not performing this act. At this point, albeit only in a successive and therefore only partial way, an Either-And-Or comes into force. This boundlessness, this freedom from commitment, must, for the sake of the commitment for which freedom must decide, be affirmed, even while it must subsequently also be negated by the very commitments freedom decides to take on.

In order to commit itself, the will must be uncommitted: liberation has to come before freedom! And liberation must come before freedom as if it were itself already freedom, to which it is, however, only the first opening, even though this opening henceforth enables not only the possibility of making use of freedom, but also every possibility of its abuse! The Either-Or in the face of caprice is followed by the Either-And-Or in the face of liberation. Where caprice's boundless freedom from commitment holds sway, there is no real freedom, which for its part, however, cannot take charge so long as there has not yet been a liberation to boundlessness, with its new-found caprice and every possible will to every sort of digressiveness.

By asking "freedom to what?" Nietzsche's Zarathustra differentiated actual and creative freedom, within whose limits the master proves him- or herself, from that "freedom from what?" which only paves the way to freedom, that is to say: merely liberates. Freedom-From-Something is, despite being no small thing and also remaining indispensable, liberation: it is the breaking free from everything that enchains one, the initial realization of this liberation and that alone. For that fruitful use which the consummated Freedom-To-Something makes of freedom—by committing itself once more of its own accord—is and can only be the act of this freedom itself, and it can only occur after liberation has also set it free to choose everything that opposes fruitfulness.

Nietzsche, however, and in this he is among those who mistrust freedom—because in order for freedom to be freedom, it must also be the freedom to abuse freedom, and because human beings have consistently and horrendously abused their freedom and continue to do so—in following the path of his correct distinction between liberation as, first of all, merely a "freedom from what?", and actual freedom as "freedom to what?", also strays from it again by succumbing to the digression of distinguishing among different types of human beings.

"There are some," says Zarathustra, "who threw away their last value when they threw away their servitude."[6] Regarding the same possible abuse of freedom, Schiller defended the more profound and accurate conviction that freedom constitutes the essence and right of every human being without exception: in the face of all subserviency a value worthy of greater esteem, no matter the circumstances!

In 1798, after nearly a decade of the at once inspiring and disconcerting French Revolution, Schiller's *Words of Faith* [*Die Worte des Glaubens*] call out to all those who are terrified by the consequences of liberation: "Do not be misled by the cry of the rabble, nor by the abuses of frenzied fools!" How to prove oneself worthy of freedom is, undeniably, something the liberated have yet to learn; and they will indeed learn, Schiller believes, if only once they have been liberated. For while there are those who, having been forced into unfreedom, are indeed "slaves," there is no such thing as slaves as such! "The human being is created free, is free, even if he were born in chains." These human beings, and that means all human beings, will come to prefer meaning to nonsense and fruitfulness to unfruitfulness, as soon as they have finally been given the chance to reach for them. And yet—because otherwise there is no freedom—choosing the opposite also becomes a constant possibility.

In this way, the message of freedom announced by the first distich of Schiller's poem heralds in—despite the reign of terror of the liberated, whose abuse of freedom can be seen running riot across the second distich—the certitude of freedom expressed in the third distich, which affirms both freedom and liberation despite liberation, no matter who or what may be set free by an act of liberation!

> The human being is created free, is free,
> Even if he was born in chains.
> Do not be misled by the cry of the rabble,
> Nor by the abuses of frenzied fools.
> Before the slave, when he breaks his chains,
> Before the free human being tremble not.

Der Mensch ist frei geschaffen, ist frei,
Und würd' er in Ketten geboren.
Laßt euch nicht irren des Pöbels Geschrei,
Nicht den Mißbrauch rasender Toren;
Vor dem Sklaven, wenn er die Ketten bricht,
Vor dem freien Menschen erzittert nicht.[7]

Freedom despite freedom

But the possible abuse of freedom that every act of liberation also sets free is not the only contradiction. Even if liberation, which must nonetheless be hazarded, were to one day become obsolete (because if everyone were free, no one would need to be liberated anymore), there would still remain, at this summit of the tried and tested Freedom-To-Something, two further contradictions, an Either-And-Or that must be sustained as indissolubly and permanently as freedom itself. It is freedom's very essence and consummation that are reflected in this twofold contradiction.

This is, first of all, because the gift of freedom places one before a task that is an occasion not only for joy but also for fear, the so-called "fear of freedom." At bottom, however, it is something other than mere fear, namely dread [*Angst*]: an anxiety that cannot be explained by anything concrete, at least not by anything worth being afraid of. Freedom is not only uplifting—and this nobody believes prior to their own liberation, although all realize it afterward—it is also a burden: the ennoblement of the self to itself is accompanied by the onerous, oppressive burden of one's personal responsibility. At the outset, before habituation (which eventually sets in here as it does everywhere) has begun to exert its moderating effect, consummated freedom weighs on one with all the ponderous gravity of the loneliness that becoming oneself, or "individuation," entails. Every human being is, becomes and remains, so that he or she might be completely him- or herself, separated from every other person, each of which embodies an other self or must strive to do so, for one's own part likewise on one's own, utterly alone unto oneself.

It should of course be pointed out that this contradiction between the satisfaction that comes from one's own power of decision, and the strain exerted by making decisions oneself and answering for them on one's own, is related to another contradiction, by virtue of which the human being first becomes a human being. The pride, the by all means justified pride in being a human being, is attended at every level of human self-development by the no less certainly contradictory humiliation of not yet being the person one is: of being held responsible, along with everything that one is, by the person one is meant to be.

But that the human being in this way shares its suffering from contradiction with other human beings—who are the sole possessors of this freedom—does not mean one suffers only half of it. In the collision that attends freedom—the collision between, on the one hand, the joy of freedom and the dread that accompanies it, and on the other hand, the internal contradiction of being a human being that is never able to attain one's own essence, even though one's essence never ceases in its demand to be attained—in this collision, each side does no more than confirm for the other the precise cause of its suffering, despite all the nonetheless inspiring magnificence of freedom and of the human being.

Every human being must answer for his or her complete freedom him- or herself and is otherwise not a complete human being. And it is only by virtue of this freedom that new goals are set, whereas one who has just been liberated to this freedom must proceed from it as if it were a goal that had already been achieved, while also bearing the following burden: freedom is not the same freedom for every human being and thus not the same freedom for all humankind. Rather, freedom is only freedom—including the freedom of humankind—when it is the freedom of every individual human being by virtue of his or her self-reliance. Dread, the shadow of this self-reliance, is unavoidable. Without it, human beings would be no better off than they would be without freedom, lacking which they— as judged according to the standard of what is essential and fruitful for them— would only be worse off, no matter what freedom might bring, including two final contradictions.

Limits of freedom—in freedom!

Ever since the final step taken by Greco-Roman antiquity at the height of its internalization of freedom came together with the Jewish step forward to messianic freedom, there has been no calm concerning the continued existence of servitude. That which all can be, namely free, they all really ought to be! This means that they should all be not merely inwardly free—whereby they may well continue to rise above their ongoing outward subjugation—but that they should and must also become free historically and together! Merely being free oneself makes one only partially free. Only once all human beings are free together will every individual also be free.

But how can all human beings be free together after humanity separates every person from every other person, so that each can be wholly him- or herself? Doesn't every freedom, once the complete freedom of a complete human being has been realized, stand in the way of the freedom of every other human being? Isn't freedom in this way driven back, and doesn't it always have to be curtailed wherever two freedoms want to expand together?

On the one hand, it is obvious that no human being is really free so long as others still are not. Regardless of whether your freedom bears you fruit only so long as you are served by others, or whether you can enjoy your freedom without having to be immediately conscious of the subjugation of others, taking advantage of it only indirectly: you are not free and nobody else is, either, so long as everyone is not.

On the other hand, the collisions between each freedom and every other freedom are all too apparent. Wouldn't it be better, after all, to prevent it from coming to such collisions? Wouldn't it, one asks oneself—downplaying as a comparatively lesser evil the challenge to one's own freedom that arises anew with the subjugation of every other—in fact be better to not acknowledge the freedom of others? Wouldn't it then at least be possible to consummate one's own freedom, or at least the freedom of some, to the extent that such consummation is nevertheless possible? The others' freedom will be taken from them again later anyway, or one will have one's own taken away, by them!

Or, and this is the abiding counterquestion: can't one freedom and another freedom set limits for themselves—of and in freedom? Doesn't freedom, understood at this height of its consummation as contradiction set free, point here even more so the way towards a collective and still liberatory path? Why shouldn't that which freedom proclaims to others—the diversity of contradictions—also apply to freedom itself?

To be sure, no one who is not yet liberated can take this final implication of freedom as seriously as it requires be taken. And no one who is not yet liberated is capable of accepting this implication prior to his or her liberation. For someone who is not yet liberated, the only thing that counts and can count is liberating oneself! Inversely, however, no one who tries to realize his or her freedom after his or her liberation can neglect the fact that freedom leads up against limits and that it can only be consummated at the price of self-limitation. What can neither be made clear to nor demanded of a person who is not yet liberated suddenly becomes apparent and is no longer difficult. The limits set at the height of consummated freedom are not chains in the sense of obstacles in the way of freedom; they are, rather, sacrifices: in the sense that they attest joyful devotion and thankfulness for one's own freedom, and confirm and reinforce this freedom precisely by doing so. Limits of freedom are—in freedom—the reinforcement of the path of freedom by means of attachment.

Now this "attachment" is not something that closes itself off, deflecting the outside and cutting itself off from within; it is, rather, an opening up that moves forward and brings joy, even though attachment commits: precisely because it does! The human being of attachment has, at the height of freedom thanks to commitment, responded to his or her other and is together with them no less free than each was alone, if not now even more free.

And in just the same way, the consummation of freedom that sets limits for itself is joy, derived from freedom and without tribulation. Just as attachment does not oppress—because it attaches by setting limits, and in doing so only enriches, that is to say, gives more than it takes and takes nothing that would not be given freely—an offering is or, rather, can and may be made of freedom, a sacrifice that—like that of love—makes all the richer the more abundantly it gives itself away.

"For you were called to freedom," Paul writes to the Galatians (5:13–14, trans. mod.), in the same sentence also hammering home the consequence of freedom, if it is to be consummated freedom: "By love serve one another!" Because you have been called to freedom, therefore by love serve one another: for the sake of freedom, and thereby realizing it. For, Paul continues, recalling the instructive commandment of the Jewish Bible—which brought to expression in an unforgettable and unsurpassable way the same process of setting limits for the sake of freedom, limits of freedom thanks to freedom—all teaching is but the fulfillment of a single word, and it is: "Love your neighbor as yourself" (Levi. 19:18).

Just as love of one's neighbor can only validate its "Yes" to the other person once it has reached the height of confirming its own self-reliance (because love of oneself is also commanded, and may not be neglected on account of love of one's neighbor, by means of whose reinforcement it, on the other hand, only consummates itself more fully), one's own consummated freedom is its own setting of limits: not as the loss of one's own consummation but precisely as its confirmation. Every freedom that sets limits for itself as it expands along its various paths thereby confirms and strengthens—if the limits are indeed limits derived from freedom—that consummation which, alongside the freedom of all other people together, is free, can be free, and will remain free.

Chapter 9

THE UNAVOIDABLE CONTRADICTION

The old meaning

"Did not fever come and smite thee, and shake thee, and cast thee down?"[1] In one of the Grimms' fairy tales, Death puts this question to his protégé, whom he had promised not to assail—at least not without warning. No one can be spared, of course, and even in his case no exception can be made. He could, however, send out his messengers before taking him, and in fact he did send his messengers. Now the protégé was falsely claiming to have been taken by surprise. "Has not gout twitched thee in all thy limbs? Did not thine ears sing? Did not tooth-ache bite into thy cheeks? Was it not dark before thine eyes? And besides all that, has not my own brother Sleep reminded thee every night of me? Didst thou not lie by night as if thou wert already dead?"[2] At a loss for words, the character in this fairy tale, titled "Death's Messengers," accepts his fate.

It has always been possible to either prepare for death or to neglect doing so; to reckon with it or to repress it; to meet it consciously or to flee from it. Yet everyone has died. Inescapably, the human being has encountered death, which fundamentally contradicts his or her life as life's coequal other. In the first historical epoch of health and illness, an epoch of countless millennia, health was therefore understood to be a condition either of illness' lack or its passing; and illness was for its part allotted to death as the bitter beginning of its sinister end. Serious illnesses were quickly deemed incurable, such that the most urgent task of the doctor was to separate those who could be healed from the chronically ill, with whom one would do better not to waste one's time.

This is, according to Plato, how Asclepius himself, the god of the healing arts, had wanted it to be. Only the naturally healthy who had a healthy way of living and whose illnesses had a foreseeable end were to be treated, and even then, only so long as they would—once restored—be able to continue living as they had before. Bodies that were already beset by disease, however, the doctor ought to refuse to gradually empty out with diet and treatment and then to fill again, because this could only lead to a long and miserable existence and—perhaps—produce progeny equally unfit for life. The true art of healing stands by the conviction that there is no need to care for those "who could not live the regular course of life." It does neither the sick themselves nor the state any good to keep alive what is already subject to death.[3]

Nursing existed nevertheless, even if it was not yet a practice of affirmative devotion to the sick because they are—curable or incurable—still complete human beings or capable of becoming such: that is to say, capable of further spiritual and intellectual growth. Only to the extent that a sick person was deemed to have an economic, political, or—occasionally, by exception—an "inherent" value, did the few who could afford a doctor remain interested enough (i.e., masters' interest in their slaves, generals' in their soldiers, caliphs' in their harem) to be concerned for their "restoration." Otherwise the hospital, to the extent that it existed at all, functioned exclusively as a "*hospitalium,*" a word that recalls the stranger as both guest [*hospes*] and enemy [*hostis*]. It was a place where one might, assuming one were not simply turned away, await one's death; a place where the starving, the thirsty and the naked, the sick and the incarcerated were all gathered together, some by force, others driven by need.

This did not change until love—the love of the biblical message—pointed out a better way, and in so doing ushered in the second historical epoch of health and illness. The sick who, owing to the doctor's helplessness, had once been expelled from the community were now to be included within it, despite the powerlessness of medicine.

Even if there was no helpful treatment and no redemptive care once a sick person's return to daily life seemed impossible, there was still, or rather, there was now for the first time, the sick visit in the proper sense. It was this act of love, of visiting the sick, that revealed the suffering human being to be one's neighbor; because everyone, including oneself, could fall ill at any moment. "Happy is he who is thoughtful of the wretched," announces one of the Psalms of David. He too shall receive support on his deathbed and healing grace on his sickbed (41:1, 2, 4). The sick suffer not only what could also befall oneself; rather, the sick suffer for one oneself, who, by being spared sickness, unjustly avoids it. It is Isaiah who is overcome by this most profound insight. "He was despised, shunned by men, a man of suffering, familiar with disease. [...] Yet it was our sickness that he was bearing" (53:3, 4).

By the age of King David, the commandment to visit the sick had become so self-evident that by pretending to be sick, David's son Amnon could make certain his father would visit him (2 Samuel 13:3,ff). And so Isaiah equates—as Jesus would several centuries later, in identifying with the suffering "servant of God"— all the "weak" with one another and with Him for the sake of whom one ought to love one's neighbor—and the foreigner—as oneself.

> Is such the fast I desire, a day for men to starve their bodies? [...] No, this is the fast I desire: to unlock the fetters of wickedness, and untie the cords of the yoke to let the oppressed go free; to break off every yoke. It is to share your bread with the hungry, and to take the wretched poor into your home; when you see the naked, to clothe him, and not to ignore your own kin (Isaiah 58:5–7).

And those would be blessed who—as Jesus also says, reinforcing the same act of love also of his own accord—had done for one of the least of his brothers what had also been done for him. "For I was hungry and you gave me food, I was thirsty and you gave me something to drink, I was a stranger and you welcomed me, I was naked and you gave me clothing, *I was sick and you visited me*, I was in prison, and you came" (Matt. 25:35–40, trans. mod., author's emphasis).

Yet the condition—the bitter and oppressively real condition of the biblical discovery of the act of love of the sick visit and of every subsequent reinforcement of its commandment—was the neglect of the sick by the state and by society in an enduring epoch of medical impotence. The sick person, that is to say, all sick people, whether poor or rich and influential or powerful, moved, as soon as their illness became serious, to the margins of the continuing lives of the healthy, who then had literally nothing but love as an impetus to treat sick people, qua dying people, with benevolence. Only modernity would usher in a new, third historical age: an epoch in which every patient is to be saved, and every disease without exception is to be treated; for all are considered to be curable in principle. This epoch has lasted until our own day, in which we can now see a fourth age emerging. This epoch will sustain the contradiction between health and sickness by recognizing the fruitfulness of existence in both conditions, as well as the possibility of life, and the reality of death, in each.

Yet for the time being, we continue to count only on returning to life, and as quickly as possible at that! We no longer suffer miserably in hospital any more than we do in our own beds, helplessly subjected to disease. Pain is stilled, or at least could be stilled, and every disease can be fought. Because the sick, given these revolutions in medicine, now count on becoming healthy again, it can even be unpleasant for them to receive visitors—in the way the sick, being sick as such, previously did—because they are now only temporarily sick. And one's visitors sense something similar. They suddenly fear that their visit will not be interpreted as an act of love undertaken out of pure devotion to their neighbor. They intend to reassure the sick person and themselves of a quick and complete recovery, but they fear their visit will call to mind the very opposite! The old meaning of illness, which was formerly—and just recently, not even two hundred years ago—a reminder of death, has been lost along with every other meaningful connection to death.

The lost meaning

This is not to question the magnificence of science, which remains a true blessing, having fathomed the causes of pain and disease as well as those of death! Science's ameliorating interventions into the causes of pain, disease, and death only reinforce how important and beneficent science is and will remain. And yet this science has been and continues to be misleading, ever since it—and its global industry—began trying to convince people that pain, as well as illness and death, can be overcome as such. While it is true that there is an anesthetic for every sort of pain, a reason for every disease and no death without a cause—the overcoming of which is therefore not merely thinkable but in fact succeeds time and again—it nonetheless remains just as true that death does not and never will cease to be unavoidable. Its coming will always be announced by pain and by illness just as it is announced by life itself—every human life without exception—no matter how healthy one may be. If the messengers of death were eliminated, their message, which signifies to human beings their mortality, would be lost, and human beings would be lost to themselves.

It is one thing to keep the messengers of death waiting by summoning all one's strength, joy, and love of life and tenaciously resisting, for both oneself and others, a pitiless death that would put an end to this life in life's very midst. To shirk death is something else entirely. To be sure, today everyone everywhere first asks—and justly so—what and who is at fault [*Schuld*] when pain cannot be stilled, when illnesses break out or when death arrives. And there should be no guilt [*Schuld*], or there should at least be no guilt in those cases where evil—an unacceptable, not an unavoidable contradiction—literally owes [*schuldet*] the good it has neglected to do. But neither death nor illness nor pain is what only a human being can be: evil instead of good. Beyond the question of fault [*Schuldfrage*], which is concerned solely with the role played by human action and inaction in causing pain, illness, and death, the question of the meaning of death arises—no less importantly—as a question about the meaning that has been lost in our time.

It is furthermore the very science of medicine that—thanks to the modern revolutions in the healing arts at the height of medicine's never before possible and thoroughly beneficial assistance—robbed not only death of every meaning, but also divested pain and disease of meaning, including, not least importantly, the sick person's own meaning. In this way, new, grievous damage was done even as medicine succeeded in redressing old injuries.

Because we no longer expect from the sick—or from hospitals—only death, and because it in fact became possible for the sick to return to life in spite of all the messengers of death, the sick person of earlier times no longer exists. This was the sick person whom the healthy, in the event that they bestirred themselves at all, relocated to the margins of their ongoing lives to die there or—at best, and if their deaths were not immediate—receive affectionate visitors. This does not mean we now have any greater understanding for the sick, however, but that now the very possibility of any ultimate understanding of the sick is being called into question. Now they live among the healthy, it's true: right in their midst! But they do not live as sick people because being sick is considered a meaningful possibility of existence in its own right, as capable of ongoing spiritual and intellectual growth and participation in civil society and the state and equal to every other form of growth and work. Rather, the sick now live alongside the healthy despite being sick, as if they were only temporarily sick, but in reality essentially healthy like everyone else. We carry on as if the sick, like all one's contemporaries and every other human being, should not and will not ever become the permanent victims of illness, that is to say, fully succumb to it; unless they die, that is, thereby resolving the question of their right to exist as sick people.

As no one challenges the right of the sick to fully participate in life, clearly the age of equality of even this possibility of existence has dawned; but it has not yet begun, because the age of modern medicine dawned at the same time.

9. The Unavoidable Contradiction

The very moment when the right to sickness was acknowledged as a condition not inferior to that of health, the recoverability of health—which medicine promises every modern person without exception—stepped into the gap. The sick therefore do not find, insofar as they are sick, the assistance, respect, and love which would allow them to effectively live and suffer in the only way they can bear fruit: with and thanks to their sickness. Rather, one discovers that one is, as a human being who is not what every person ought to be—namely healthy—on leave in order to be "treated" until one has "recovered." To be sure, one's rights are still acknowledged, and this certainly does constitute a cataclysmic achievement, which we will take up again later. But these rights are only acknowledged to the extent that the sick are healthy rather than sick. To insist on one's rights is to do so on the condition that one is either completely healthy or healthy again, or that one will be healthy as soon as the illness has been "overcome." As a sick person one does not participate—one's undisputed "leave" notwithstanding—in communal life: not even on the margins of it.[4]

Ever since the modern science of medicine learned to effectively intervene in every cause of pain, sickness, and death without exception, the hospital and the doctors with their medical research and medical treatment have been playing more important roles than ever before, while the sick no longer play any role at all. Everything—including the sick—turns on health. Health is "served" by those who and that which serve the sick, and the sick likewise serve health. It is the only remaining court of judgment, and human beings, so that they can give testimony of it, sacrifice themselves to it as if their life, if it is the life of a sick person, were no life at all and as if the life of a healthy person were a life without pain: both of which would indeed be the case were it not for the dying that is to come. While the origins of such callousness are no mystery, it is nonetheless incomprehensible that, intoxicated by the health cult's maxim of living life to the hilt and the supposedly ever-abiding possibility of being restored to flourishing health, human suffering—which is still as lonesome, miserable, bitter, and torturous as ever before—is either not registered at all or else not acknowledged as a self-sufficient, permanent, and creative possibility of existence.

For a humanity that has shirked the message broadcast by pain and sickness, even the messengers have lost their meaning. They will only become significant again once their contradiction, which they have gone on announcing nonetheless, again overtakes life at the height of science—in a collision potentially more deadly than any before.

The enduring meaning

Prior to any disavowal or answering of the question of meaning raised by death and its messengers, we are confronted with the unavoidable end of life as a fourfold necessity.

In the biological-ontological context, death constitutes the price for the precious gift of "higher life" enjoyed by all highly individuated plants and animals as well as human beings; not as their life's ruination—although it may appear so to one immediately affected by death—but as their life's greatest triumph. In order to get beyond the single cell, the fundamental building block of all life, and advance to the comprehensive and complex structures at the elaborate pinnacle of which a human being emerged, asexual reproduction, knowing only duplication, and nothing of death, first had to be overcome. There was no other way out of the cul-de-sacs in which asexual reproduction, with its unbridled multiplication of hereditary defects, is eventually trapped at higher levels of articulation. But this also meant accepting death. The structures that now shared and mixed their genetic material had to be dismantled again so that they—in supplementing each other—could also reciprocally rein each other in once they had reproduced in this way. The life they begat joined them, and alongside it they became superfluous and literally "outlived" themselves to the extent that they dared remain alive longer than required for passing on their vitality and their genetic material. At the same time, however, this venture of living on without fulfilling any biological purpose bore its own unique fruit: love.

Owing to this additional gift, death for the first time took on the bitter taste it has for the living creature that has become a human being, but it also revealed once more the triumph of "higher life"—which it again consummates—in a more joyful way than death itself can disclose. At the level of reproduction, the previous asexual form is replaced by one in which counterparts have to mutually seek out, find, and—once their offspring begin to require their care after birth—hold on to one another. In this opening, the human being becomes accessible to itself as husband and wife, and an attachment becomes possible that carries them both beyond the life with which they reproduce and beyond the death that marks the end of their life. In that sublime hour in which ascendant life, advancing towards the soul and the spirit, accepted death in order to bring forth the human being, love too bestowed itself upon this human being: this love that must accept the superior power of death in order to unfold—"fierce as death"—in spite of it, just as death must accept the superior power of love. "Its darts are darts of fire, a blazing flame. Vast floods cannot quench love, nor rivers drown it" (Song 8:6–7).

Giambattista Vico's pioneering *New Science of the Common Nature of Peoples* was therefore right to draw attention to the fact that all peoples everywhere without exception have three features in common, regardless of the spatial and temporal distances separating them and no matter how they were founded: a faith, wedding celebrations, and funerals. "[A]ll bury their dead."[5] And they give up, we must add nearly two and a half centuries after Vico, their humanity and their human dignity as soon as they lose their strength to commit in the face of love and as soon as they lose their respect for the deceased in the face of death. The trenchant meaning of death and love is perhaps most powerfully expressed in the way human beings of all times have valued—above all else—the observance of strict formal rules for laying out and taking leave of the deceased, on the one hand, and the strictness of ultimate commitments, including oaths of inviolable fidelity and indissoluble union, on the other. It is not these forms, but only themselves that they will condemn if they should one day no longer be equal to the literally deadly seriousness of the one process or to the seriousness of the other one whereby death is overcome.

Furthermore, in the psychological-anthropological context death constitutes the dark side of the breakthrough to the ego, which can only temporarily elude the cycle of nature from which its individuality willfully steps forth. "Whence the manifold being in totality has its coming into being, there it also passes away according to necessity," Anaximander taught in this "oldest saying of Western thinking."[6] "Each thus atones and pays a penalty for its 'dis-order' [*Un-fug*] (as Heidegger accurately translates it here, instead of speaking of injustice [*Ungerechtigkeit*] as Nietzsche does, or of dastardliness [*Ruchlosigkeit*] like Diels), according to the ordinance of time." And yet the human being succeeds, literally simultaneously, in integrating this harsh necessity—which demands for the gift of life the gift of death in return—into its life by creatively concentrating its individuality into a uniqueness of the soul that in death does not merely forfeit what it was but instead irrevocably consummates what it was precisely by dying—after a meaningful life—a meaningful death worthy of that life.

Dying, at first a primarily biological event, has also become so thoroughly personal a process that human beings must, for the sake of their peace of mind, find meaning in it; at the same time, one can decide whether and when—according to the measure of this meaning—one no longer wants to acquiesce in the life one finds oneself born into. Whereby one must in either case also acquiesce in the fact that death relieves one of this decision about one's life—against one's will! Psychically, too, death looms, even if the person to whom the psyche belongs, and his or her body, are neither exhausted to death nor yet prepared to die.

On the one hand, human beings have made death their own to such an extent that they are free to specify to this unavoidable adversary, who will sooner or later do away with them, the hour of their own elimination—whereby they however put themselves in "deadly" peril in a new way. The thoroughly creative possibility of a genuinely free death [*Freitod*] for political, economic, physical, or other reasons, which older societies and a number of ancient states officially granted to individuals who applied on such grounds, has now become a seduction to mere suicide. The escapism, obsession, confusion, and groundlessness of suicide pose the constant threat of—infectious—mental illness, of a terrifying epidemic that must be prevented and treated with all available means. Suicides must be distinguished clearly from those who choose death in genuine freedom, those who have and retain the right to dispose over their life, and who contribute more than one more positive meaning to the abundance of meanings contained in martyrdom, in which the sacrifice of one's own life is that life's very fulfillment.

On the other hand, people who do not die from physical, so to speak "external" causes which overcome them or which they bring upon themselves, die from psychological causes from "within," even when the art of healing overcomes all the physical causes of their dying. To not die when the time has come is no less painful than the prospect, within life, that one must die. In this way death, now in the guise of the soul's own and actual passing away—just as its body's life ends as soon as it has "outlived" itself—is all the more welcome to the soul the more completely it was able to immediately "live life" or process in a mediate way what complicated, impeded, or made superfluous its "enjoyment" of life, it too a soul "living life" to the hilt. If it is written that Abraham, Isaac, David, and not least Job died, and then for good, only once they were "full" of life (Gen. 25:8; 35:29; 1 Chr. 29:28; Job 42:17), it is in order to celebrate their passing as death at the height of the soul's consummation, whose highest and literally permanent fulfillment is not survival, as if this were possible, but rather death: the supremely meaningful ending of life at the end of every meaningful continuation of life as life and as the life of the soul.

Thirdly, there is a deep and essential anchoring of death in the relationship of the messengers of death and of death itself to the spirit. From the very beginning, it is neither the individual life that has progressed to the spirit nor the uniqueness of that life—its soul—that is truly at stake here. In constituting the lawfulness in all human beings and in the All, the spirit is, on the one hand, only ever grasped in but one of its instantiations; yet in precisely this way, the personal power of spirit of this singular instantiation also makes clear, and itself understands, that it itself is not what matters when, and to the extent that, the individual embodies spirit. The supra-individual essence of truth and the fact of such knowability of the world point beyond the vessel of reason that mirrors it, and beyond death, which sooner or later mercilessly shatters the mirror of every vessel of reason. As only the *eternal transformation* of matter otherwise can, spirit at the height—and in the depth—of its *immutable eternity* mocks death, which—between "matter" as the raw material of existence in the former case and "reflection" as the elevation of the spirit to contemplation in the latter—can only kill life and obliterate the soul. It is neither one's life nor one's soul, but rather the matter and the spirit in which all human beings take part and always can take part more profoundly, that enables them, too, to mock death: freely, cheerfully, and full of confidence.

The human being, the embodiment of living matter, finds him- or herself subject to death only as the life of matter; but as the substance of this life, one is exempt from death, just as one is, with one's living soul that must breathe its last, strong in spirit—that is to say, immortal each time one's spirit ascends to the summit of consciousness to attain the height that is also the height of knowledge of one's own mortality. "Death has been swallowed up in victory," writes Paul, and justly so, to the Corinthians, with express reference to Hosea's "Where, O Death, are your plagues? Your pestilence where, O Sheol?" (Hos. 13:14). Paul continues: "Where, O death, is your victory? Where, O death, is your sting?" (1 Cor. 15:54–55).

It is not life in its flourishing, but rather death in its menacing that unites—and allies—us with the spirit. A life is devoid of spirit, no matter how "inspired" it may present itself, if while riding the cresting waves of its full vigor and enjoyment it fails to hear the messengers of death, represses them, or perhaps insists, on account of what is eternal in and about itself, that it need not heed the message that not only pain, suffering, and sickness invoke, but which is also invoked by health and by life itself, capable as they are of coming to an end out of the blue at any time. Whoever on the other hand—and not only in the wave troughs of his or her existence—is prepared to endure pain, because life, and above all "higher life," only broke through—and only can break through—to love by way of mortality, and because life attains the life of the soul only at the price of its suffering, has spirit. For this as for a thousand other reasons, the healthy need the sick.

For it is first of all the sick, and only after them the healthy who stand by them—assuming they do not stand by the suffering merely out of pity and self-pity—who bear powerful witness, against the bruisers and vitalist vulgarians, of the essence and power of that spirit that suffers and loves for all. "Out of his anguish he shall see it; [...] by his insight he will bring justice to many," Isaiah thus says (53:11) upon his discovery of the vicarious suffering of those who are familiar with illness. Or, to use a current expression about the "limits of medicine": "*Sick people are alive too!*"[7]

Yet it would be wrong, fundamentally wrong, to thus equate spirit with illness, suffering or pain, as if these were necessary conditions of its existence, as if the spirit—as this line of thinking goes—could not exist without the messengers of death. Spirit is no less an uplifting and meaningful expression of healthy existence; yet existence finds it difficult to take a step back from itself as long as its health is not called into question. It is thus only too often that the human being first becomes conscious of the spirit from the perspective of that future farewell recalled to him or her—in life, and as soul—by the messengers of death! But the spirit, this lawfulness in everything and in each one and in the All, merely resonates in response to being called forth by their message as that which is superior even to itself. Always, and in view of everything there is, capable of learning—like one who knows that he or she knows and can bring his or her knowledge to bear on consciousness—every human being embodies, in health as well as in sickness, spirit as the consciousness of his or her reason beyond all experiences also included in the knowledge of the animal, and all insights comprehended by the understanding: "the kind of being," says Max Scheler, which "can take an ascetic attitude toward life."[8]

Fourthly, and to judge now on principle, in philosophy's own name: the unavoidable contradiction of death—from which the human being as substance and as spirit is exempt, but to which it succumbs in life and as a soul—places us also before the contradiction whose explosion of unity through diversity does not cut the All off from its totality but rather makes totality available to it completely for the first time. Like the human being unto itself: complete! Not only temporarily or incidentally, and by no means disparagingly, but rather "in principle" and for the good, the human being can, as Scheler puts it, conduct him- or herself ascetically and thereby bear fruit precisely because he or she is a person "who can say 'No.'"[9]

Thanks to its spirit and thus anything but "negativistically," but rather thoroughly creatively, for good—and very good—reasons, the human being rises above its existence, from life to the life of the soul. Out of commitment to these reasons, each human being must, upon arriving at death, register but a further "no"—which is in this case the negation of him- or herself—for reasons that are no less good, but are indeed very good. That which evil alone and only evil represents—unacceptable contradiction—is something entirely different from death, whose inevitability must instead be accepted "according to the ordinance of time"[10] and can also be accepted almost, or even sincerely, gratefully—despite being most decisively rejected at the same time. It was wrong of Paul, who, as a disciple of Hosea, robbed death of its sting to, in another discipleship to which he was committed, play death off against the "law" and amalgamate it with evil: "The sting of death is sin" (1 Cor. 15:56).

Evil and evil alone—or sin, to put it in theological terms—is what death is not: contradiction without any good reason. As explainable and perhaps even desirable as it may be in biological and psychological terms, evil remains literally inexcusable, so that an ultimately exclusively good world without guilt and guilty people is capable of being thought as well as built, in a struggle against evil. An exclusively healthy world without the messengers of death and without death is, on the contrary, neither capable of being thought or worth building, and the same is true for a world in which only sickness would rule, with death as the only master. A good and—one day—exclusively good world of struggle against evil is a still human world. A world only of the healthy, however, rid completely of suffering and pain, would be inhuman; along with sickness and the sick, it would have done away with the human being itself. The fact that life and its ego and self, the soul, must die is only half of their truth. They die because they live, and both facts are true, in contradiction to each other.

The reclaimed meaning

No matter how often the messengers of death again catch up with us—whether in the body, which is, thanks to the science of medicine, more transparent than ever; or in the soul, which, owing to "depth psychology," we now understand with greater clarity than was previously possible; or in the twentieth century's global theaters of war; or even in traffic (itself another theater of war, or an even more murderous substitute for one), where the messengers of death make a bountiful killing and are no less impossible to overlook than they are in every place where hunger and misery are on the rise as never before despite reasoned economic policies and the leadership of science, or in all the places where unbridled technology is destroying culture along with nature—there suddenly appears, once again, a means of shirking the unavoidability of renewed reflection on the meaning of death.

Indeed, it is only ever the individual human being who dies, even when hundreds of thousands or millions die together. But this does not mean the individual is the only one who is sick, as the one who happens to be singled out in each particular instance; rather, society itself is also sick. Individuals are destroyed just as often or even more often by groups—intimate ones, small ones, larger constellations, the state, and the community of states—as they destroy themselves.

It was thus an authentic and revolutionary innovation, the importance of which can hardly be exaggerated, that social existence as such came to be integrated into the struggle for health. But at the same time, this also created an expectation that society could be as completely curable and healable as modernity had once promised the individual it could become. As if these individuals had not already been shamefully deceived by this expectation, it seemed to them at the proud height of their design of the modern world—where they do still become sick, feel pain, suffer, and are subject to death—as if it were not up to them, but rather dependent upon society how sick or healthy they and other people are, and whether these others and they themselves must die.

And to be sure, it is not only the illnesses that were treated in previous ages that should be cured if they are curable and—if they are not—integrated, along with the sick themselves, into the lives of those who are spared their sickness, in full affirmation of their existence. Wounded soldiers, too, victims of war in the "classical" sense of its waging, deserve the same degree of attention, as does the home country, which, no longer a "hinterland" on the grounds of modernity, is hit in a most unclassical way almost even harder by war, not to mention the prisoners of war and all prisoners whatsoever. Even so, we have mentioned only a fraction of all those struck by the pain, suffering and illnesses behind which death lies in wait.

> Today there are the victims of the environmental crisis—incalculably "wounded" by stench, pollution, noise pollution, toxins, traffic and other dangers—or, to mention at least two further examples, there are the victims of displaced "social costs" and the victims of large and small-scale business, who either lack consumer protections or whom they can hardly help, owing to lack of means.[11]

Just as it previously proved possible to provide medical care to all those who were sick in the classical sense, and to care for the victims of war in the narrow and broader sense of the term, whose reintegration into life remains a major accomplishment of modernity that was and is by no means to be taken for granted, looking after the socially wounded ought to also be, or become, a matter of course: by healing the society that mutilates them! In addition to the victims of war and all the sick in the older sense of *Wounded in the First Degree* there is thus also, as I concluded a lecture on the *Philosophy of Society* in January 1974, "the *Wounded in the Second Degree*, including every physically, psychologically or spiritually injured human being without exception. It does not help one much to merely stay alive. One can only be helped by a society which in the future injures neither human beings nor human dignity."[12]

But even then, our—most beneficial—comprehension of the countless causes of pain and suffering, and of the causes of death of the countless victims of social conditions that call out for society itself to be cured, can do nothing at all to change the fact that without death, there would be no life, nor any life of the soul either, and that neither would be what they are if they were not simultaneously damned to one day no longer be. Certainly, this condition is not the only one that counts as health, but it too *is health*: keeping faith with life when surrounded by the messengers of death! On the other hand, living a life free of pain and being glad of it, but not wanting to suffer, let alone to die, is not a healthy state even where, as seen from without, health still predominates; it is, rather, stupidity, a state of mental illness that is more infectious, more dangerous and graver than the majority of all "real" diseases taken together.

But we have been facing the threat of this thoroughly diseased condition, of desiring to be healthy and nothing but healthy because every illness without exception is supposed to be curable, ever since the Good News of the third historical age of health and illness—which promised a treatment for every illness without exception—reached the developing countries, on the one hand, and the masses of the industrial world on the other. What a fateful imbrication! Just when the leading strata of the industrialized countries and their immense medical complex, including representatives of technology and science and—even—business, which profited and continues to profit, are beginning to seriously acknowledge the limits at which growth—not in the sense of what will henceforth be its qualitative growth, but growth in the sense of quantitative proliferation—should be reined in, this proliferation begins to be demanded on a global scale. Nonetheless, the only truly progressive path is the one that was initiated by the fourth historical age of health and illness. In affirming the freedom of each of these mutually contradictory modes of existence—and despite the fact that they contradict each other—it nonetheless presupposes a much more just distribution of access to the healing arts than what is now in evidence, and in this respect it is also devoted to quantitative growth. For every curable illness, it should be possible to find the doctor who can cure it, and everyone who can heal should be admitted to the sick person who requires his or her help: and this should not be restricted to just one—the highest—level of training in the healing arts!

The human being, like humankind, which is made up of human beings whom society goes on outliving until even its own "eternal" structures are either dissolved by its own dynamic or dismantled by "posterity" or its neighbors, reclaims its meaning at that point, and only at that point, where death inescapably calls it into question. It is characteristic of meaning that it can also be given, and not merely found. Life that assumes its existence as something more than its own personal existence, and devotes itself to it, has meaning if and because it pays for its beginning with its end. None of the cures that hold the messengers of death at bay, or hold off death itself, should be underestimated, but neither should their power be overestimated. Love is fierce as death.

The fourth historical age of health and illness, an age in which contradiction is set free in this area as well, unites the healthy, who are never merely healthy, with the sick, who never need to be merely sick, in the same affirmation of life, suffering and dying. Life thus remains meaningful all the way into death, regardless of how healthy or sick one may be: fruitful in health and fruitful in sickness, and vitally important in both.

Chapter 10

THE UNACCEPTABLE CONTRADICTION

Guilt and exculpation

What is evil?

Is evil the opposite of the good—a mere opposite that complements the good and forecloses it at the same time? That is to say, is evil merely the alternative to the good? Or is evil in its conflict with the good the latter's contradiction, such that good and evil call each other irreconcilably into question, meaning they are both also—precisely because they call each other into question—to be accepted? Or is evil, rather, the occurrence of guilt on top of the alternatives and conflicts that entertain evil? In that case evil—and only evil—would be what no other contradiction is, that is to say, unacceptable: an unacceptable contradiction!

Here the very first biblical usage of the word "sin" remains instructive in a pathbreaking way, where it is said to Cain prior to his fratricide: "Why are you distressed? And why is your face fallen? Surely, if you do right, there is uplift. But if you do not do right sin couches at the door; its urge is toward you, yet you can be its master" (Gen. 4:6–7).

This illustrates evil and its consequences in an exemplary, matter-of-fact way that is also remarkably untheological and above all precisely accurate. Evil appears along with the good, in view of which it proves itself to be evil, not at a crossroads but rather—together with the good—along one and the same path, which the good masters and from which evil deviates. It is literally the misstep, the aberrant detour: going astray! This is why a threat arises here, the threat posed to Cain, which indeed differentiates a person who gives in to evil from one who resists it. A person walking the straight path of the good is literally and figuratively "upright" as well as relatively calm, cheerful, and free, yet a person who has left the straight path is angry and downcast: restless yet gloomy under a dark weight.

The cause of this burden is guilt: that is, the outstanding debt of good always owed by evil. But—as is often argued these days—and by no means in denial of the new, modern scale of evil with its once unthinkable cold-bloodedness and unimaginable lack of restraint: is guilt real? And even if it were! Wouldn't guilt still always be excusable, that is to say, acceptable? This is how psychology and biology speak, these generally convincing, relentlessly progress-oriented sciences. They deny neither evil as such nor its modern excess. Yet they literally ex-culpate it.

Psychology teaches that without evil there is no good. Were it not for the drive, the embodiment of all psychic energy, not only evil actions but also the good actions that resist evil would be impossible. Aggression, itself a consequence of social conditions by which it finds itself almost unavoidably provoked, is not simply a bad thing, without which a better life would be possible. It is, rather, life itself: the condition not only of evil—or of so-called evil—but also of the good, whether real or merely so-called. Human consciousness and its resistance to evil represent only a fraction of what an entire human being really is: unconscious and subconscious existence in addition to consciousness. The unconscious remains at least partially accessible to consciousness, whereas the subconscious is and remains impenetrable.

So this, as biology confirms in taking up the narrative here as well, is finally our entire reality: unconscious and subconscious behavior constituting all human activity. Without nature there is no culture. The development to a human being remains a part—and is a mere fraction—of the plant and animal existence that human beings only recently left not very far behind and to which they remain subject in the form of instinct.

And in two respects psychology and biology are absolutely right, although they are prefigured by a remark of Paul's that has gone carelessly neglected by the exaggerated self-consciousness and hasty optimism of the last centuries. "Not what I want do I carry out, I do rather what I hate [...] For it is not the good that I want that I do, but rather the evil that I do not want that I do" (Rom. 7:15 and 19, trans. modified). It is not enough to merely want the good, let alone to merely command it. The authoritarianism of mastery and the call to mastery from above, whose tragic effects are still being felt, misunderstand not only the essence of human beings—which they overhastily equate with the good, or at least the possible realization of the good—but also the essence of the difficulty with which human beings must acknowledge evil in order to be capable of resisting it.

Completely in the right in the face of all such misleading commandments from on high, psychology and biology unleash a rebellion from below, as whose advance guard they are again completely in the right, yet without therefore being immune to making misleading suggestions in their own right. Men like Freud, Darwin, Marx, Nietzsche, and not least Einstein, this pioneer of the physical unleashing of the material "underworld," represent an overthrowing of all previous forms of rule in which what was once repressed, oppressed, and exploited by those forms of rule is ushered back into the light of day, as into a finally complete All. Here, too, Paul is right when he writes to the Romans, in illustration of Christianity's relationship to Jewry: "It is not you that support the root, but the root that supports you" (Rom. 11:18).

But is that all there is to it?

Even those who have, after it was neglected for so long, given us a deeper understanding of evil by pointing it out and then going on to exculpate it either fully or in part, insist on human particularities. They hold that human beings are, despite being animated by the drive and bound by instinct, something essentially different than animals. Human beings are also consciousness, which is to say, responsible. Psychology and biology may either accept or doubt that human beings can live up to their responsibility. But they too agree that human beings indeed have a unique responsibility.

For the guilt of the human being is neither mere evil in opposition to the good in an eternal balancing act of good and evil, nor is it the always unavoidable occasion of a "natural" conflict. Rather, guilt is the debt of good "owed" by every act of evil, a misdeed and literal mis-deed [*Un-Tat*], which should not have been performed and most certainly need not be performed. Guilt owes what it repents on the grounds of culture, where it plays a major role: a far, far greater one than the supposedly natural law of the balance of good and evil would like to admit.

In tormenting itself just as it torments its victims, evil develops into a corrosive agony of ever more evil. But this does not exclude the possibility of evil thereby faring as well as Job and the 73rd Psalm are forced to concede.

> Such are the wicked;
> Ever tranquil, they amass wealth. [...]
>
> Their bull breeds and does not fail;
> Their cow calves and never miscarries;
> They let their infants run loose like sheep,
> And their children skip about.
> They sing to the music of timbrel and lute,
> And revel to the tune of the pipe;
> They spend their days in happiness,
> And go down to Sheol in peace. (Ps. 73:12; Job 21:10–13)

But this very real enjoyment of life by the wicked, up to and including a restful, peaceful end despite their guilt, alters nothing about the fact that guilt is the good that is owed and that evil is the neglected good, whereas the good is a value in itself. Neither does the far greater pervasiveness of evil in relation to good, nor the no less real existential hardship and deprivation of the good, down to the very real suffering of the innocent. That which evil is not and can never be, no matter how much power, splendor, fame, or so-called success it boasts, the good is always: valuable, no matter how impotent and lackluster it may be in comparison, no matter how devoid of fame and success.

Evil never does and never can triumph over good, as its guilt attests time and again, for it never suffices unto itself. Yet this is what the good is: sufficient unto itself. Here there is no failing; nothing is neglected, no matter how poorly the good may fare; even in the worst case its good is only not yet good enough. For blessedness is, as the immortal last proposition of Spinoza's *Ethics* concisely and correctly states, "not the reward of virtue, but virtue itself."[1]

Guilt and Turning

Because they owe the good, the failings of evil that emerge from the psychic economy and balance of psychology, and from the bodily economy and balance of biology, create a burden of guilt. In this way, evil also constitutes the foundation for two human particularities that are as humiliatingly oppressive as they are blissfully uplifting—along with a third particularity, a unique, liberating opportunity that is open to human beings and to human beings alone.

There is conscience and there is regret, which—because they exist and can be taught, but are never merely taught—also prove for their part that evil is something more than the opposite of the good, something in itself, namely guilt. It makes no difference how excusable this guilt may be according to psychology and biology, nor even how "wholeheartedly" it may be "forgiven," as it is commonly put. One's own conscience remains nonetheless all too aware of its evil, an ongoing, nagging occasion of bitter, most bitter regret. Such that in time, which does not heal the wound, evil proves, according to the degree of one's conscious realization of its departure from the good, to be a burden that increases rather than decreases. Simultaneously, however, another possibility arises here nonetheless, an opportunity for liberation from this burden—and a solid, unshakable occasion for true joy.

For with conscience and thanks to regret, we eventually arrive at the further, on the one hand only more terribly oppressive, but on the other hand also more blissfully uplifting event of Turning. This Turning is available to every guilty person without exception, and from every guilt without exception.

The biblical concept of Turning [*teshuva*]—similarly to the concept of sin, which refers literally to the "transgression" [*Vor-Gang*] that it denounces—summons to a Turning from the detour of the good's neglect and to nothing else. But in the context of Christianity, first by way of its translations into Greek, the concept came to signify a largely internalized Turning in the sense of a change of heart; in German this later became penance [*Buße*].[2] But as penance, this biblical Turning, which joyfully proclaims the possibility, and everyone's possibility, of turning away from guilt, carries a predominant connotation of penal law: hardly uplifting, much more oppressive and apparently also a disgrace. Yet Turning is good news through and through, to no one's dishonor. "Repent!" (Matt. 3:2; 4:17), meaning "Turn around!" is how the gospel, literally the "Good News," begins (Isa. 61:1). From its origin in biblical prophecy, this good news had 600 years previously also become the message of Judaism and has remained an exhilarating assurance of undiminished promise ever since.

> Repent and turn around
> from your transgressions;
> [...]
> and get yourselves a new heart and a new spirit,
> that you may not die,
> O House of Israel.
> For it is not My desire
> that anyone shall die—
> declares the Lord God.
> Turn, therefore, and live! (Ezek. 18:30–32)

10. The Unacceptable Contradiction

In the new situation of the Babylonian exile, after the destruction of their state and temple—a loss to which no other ancient people was able to respond with renewed historical impact—Ezekiel became the spokesman for his Jewish people as they were arising again and proving their resilience. His teaching was this: never and nowhere does the guilt of the fathers preclude the Turning of their sons, just as the guilt of the sons never and nowhere prevents the Turning of their fathers.

But Ezekiel also distinguishes himself from the social prophets of the pre-exilic period of Jewry, as Hermann Cohen writes in his superb chapter on *Atonement*, by establishing sin as "the sin of the individual and in that he discovers in sin the individual."[3] Turning, be it that of the sons or that of the fathers: their Turning and every Turning is a personal achievement! Everyone can, everyone must accomplish Turning on his or her own, for him- or herself. The doctrine that had already been developed by Isaiah—that there is something left over when one turns, a vestige that remains and that will, because one turns, remain (10:20–22; 11:11, 16)—is stepped up from being a message addressed to the people as a collective to being a message of renewal addressed to individuals, first to the individual members of this people and then to the individual members of all peoples whatsoever.

> A child shall not share the burden of a parent's guilt,
> nor shall a parent share the burden of a child's guilt;
> the righteousness of the righteous shall be accounted to him alone,
> and the wickedness of the wicked shall be accounted to him alone.
> Moreover, if the wicked one repents
> of all the sins that he committed
> and keeps all My laws
> and does what is just and right,
> he shall live;
> he shall not die.
> None of the transgressions he committed
> shall be remembered against him;
> because of the righteousness he has practiced,
> he shall live. (Ezek. 18:20–22)

In opening up and affirming the future, this captures the essential core of ethical life in its entirety. The human being awakes between good and evil and goes forth from them, and because of them, as a responsible individual. Yet at the same time, all individuals share the same good and evil. Just as false as the monisms involved in interpreting the All as an either purely good or purely evil world is the dualism that divides the All into the worlds of exclusively evil people on the one side and exclusively good people on the other.

In contrast to the "ethos" of personal normativity and to the "morality" of socially required normativity, there is "ethics"—the one and only normativity shared by all human beings of all peoples at the height of their awakening to individuality. As important as the diversity of ethos and the immeasurable plurality of possible moralities otherwise are, they are of no consequence in the face of this ethics, which in addition to founding individuality also creates new bonds between individuals. Such that in addition to each individual's personal guilt, there is also one's part in complicity [*Mitschuld*]: the way one is immediately affected by all the guilt of all guilty people without exception. That is why bringing about the Turning of every guilty person is not only a possibility, but also a duty alongside the possibility and duty of one's own Turning. Just as every person can waken the conscience of every other person (of which no one can be relieved), every person can also move every other person to a Turning. The book of Jonah was the first to bear witness, and already in a radical way, to the triumph of this responsibility for one another.

Even for Nineveh, "that great city" (3:2–3) which for Jonah was not only far off in the most foreign of lands, but also the capital of the enemies of his people, Turning is a possibility, and Nineveh indeed turns. "The people of Nineveh believed God. They proclaimed a fast, and great and small alike put on sackcloth" (3:5). Not even Jesus can paint a picture that goes further than this. "The sign of Jonah" (Matt. 12:39; 16:4) remains a revolutionary touchstone; there is no greater warning or better example of Turning. "The people of Nineveh," he says, "shall rise up at the judgment with this generation and condemn it, because they repented at the proclamation of Jonah" (Matt. 12:41). They repented, that is: they turned. And so it happened:

> God saw what they did,
> how they were turning from their evil ways.
> And God renounced the punishment
> he had planned to bring upon them,
> and did not carry it out. (3:10, trans. mod.)

The good of Turning

Yet as soon as Turning becomes a conscious possibility in addition to guilt, and since every guilty person without exception can turn from every guilt without exception, the possibility of Turning also has a seductive effect at first, functioning as no less than an invitation to guilt. Wouldn't it now be possible to do evil, since its guilt has no finality, but is rather only a precursor to the final step of Turning? Yet an answer to this was recorded early on in the Jewish tradition: "If someone says he wants to sin, and the day of reconciliation will expiate it, then the day of reconciliation does not expiate it." And: "One's sins against one's neighbors are not expiated by the day of reconciliation until one has placated one's neighbor."[4]

For Turning, a mere change of one's own heart does not suffice, and betting on the future possibility of Turning suffices even less, in the event that not even a real change of heart has occurred. And even if it has occurred, and has already led to the guilty person's aiming for good, even doing good does not suffice in the case of those who have not also rectified their former evil. The absolute necessity of having made reparations is already connected to Turning by Ezekiel (33:14–16). Justice and truth must take the place of injustice and falsehood, but something more must also occur so that the sins committed by the guilty person are no longer attributed to him or her. That which was seized must be returned; that which was stolen must be repaid!

But then, when this "complete Turning" is accomplished, when "a person accomplishes a complete Turning, such that his heart is uprooted within him," then Turning succeeds in opening up a new path of ethical progress that is superior even to the paths of those whose good spares them a Turning from evil. "There, where those accomplishing their Turning stand," at the ethical peak climbed by their Turning—says Rabbi Abbahu, whose teaching blossomed around 300—"the perfectly just are unable to stand." And in a pointed passage of the gospel that is only so seldomly disconcerting because it is hardly ever taken as seriously and literally as intended, Jesus teaches exactly the same thing. The turning sinner, Jesus teaches here, even one sinner who turns, brings more joy than ninety-nine of the just who have no need of Turning.

For Jesus, who hereby continues the Jewish tradition he inherited, and in an especially precise way at that by remaining within the framework of the parables of the lost sheep and faithful shepherd developed by Isaiah (40:11) and Ezekiel (34: 11 and 16), says in Luke (15:4–7):

> Which one of you, having a hundred sheep and losing one of them, does not leave the ninety-nine in the wilderness and go after the one that is lost until he finds it? When he has found it, he lays it on his shoulders and rejoices. And when he comes home, he calls together his friends and neighbors, saying to them, "Rejoice with me, for I have found my sheep that was lost." Just so, I tell you, there will be more joy in heaven over one sinner who repents than over ninety-nine righteous persons who need no repentance.[5]

Yet this close connection between guilt and Turning nonetheless does not mean that they are one and the same. Between guilt, and Turning from guilt, lies the same abyss that differentiates good and evil, despite the "And" between them. Despite all the good promised by Turning, this Turning from evil: evil itself is not therefore any less evil; it is still only guilt. Even though it had to be committed so that Turning could turn away from it, it nonetheless should not have been committed!

That which, time and again, makes what is right about the modern excuses for guilt into a wrong, namely the fact that they—whose psychological and biological insights provide a correct and essential supplement—try to divorce evil from guilt, as if the evil they excuse were therefore less guilty or even no guilt at all, never posed and still does not pose any danger to the connection between Turning and guilt. There is nothing wrong with speaking of "guilt and Turning" in one breath, as joyfully as can be—and justifiably joyfully at that!—rather than speaking of guilt alone. The fact and bitter truth that evil is wicked, and that guilt is evil, is not hereby called into question.

In the end only good!

To acknowledge guilt as guilt—that it is a good owed—and to denounce evil as the evil of failing to do the good that it owes, constitutes the first step on the path to Turning and the first stirring of every ethics. With it, a human being furthermore sets out on the path to him- or herself, a human being, and to him- or herself as a self. The historical period of the individual begins only thanks to, and as a result of, taking on this personal responsibility for the evil of guilt.

At the same time, the individual human being who, in the face of his or her guilt and by means of his or her conscience and regret, breaks open and sets off on the path to his or her Turning, becomes aware, to his or her encouragement and burden, of his or her connection with all human beings everywhere, through additional guilt. The evil of one's own guilt is joined by the evil of complicity, which amplifies personal responsibility into collective responsibility. From an ethical perspective, of course, each can judge only him- or herself, "[f]or with the judgment you make you will be judged, and the measure you give will be the measure you get" (Matt. 7:2). This truth and this warning cannot be repeated often enough! But the fact that, ethically speaking, each can judge only him- or herself does not free anyone from the responsibility of making the guilty aware of their guilt or from bringing their guilt, should it involve an adjudicable crime, before a court of justice. And it especially does not free anyone from the knowledge that they are complicit in another's guilt.

The good of Turning can only proceed beyond the evil of guilt when the Turning, which acknowledges all the evil of which the individual knows itself to be directly guilty, also acknowledges itself to be complicit in all the guilt of every guilty person in the entire world.

Acknowledging guilt in this way, from the guilt of one's own evil to complicity in all evil whatsoever, also means, in the form of this acknowledgment of guilt: standing up to guilt! Evil is, unlike every other contradiction, unacceptable: absolutely not to be tolerated! In responding to guilt, Turning doesn't merely pay it a visit in order to admit it to itself or to hold a mirror up to others. Rather—assuming one hasn't merely imposed oneself as judge without having judged oneself—it rises up against guilt by acknowledging its own and every other's guilt.

What seems like little, if not all too little—and again seems like little when the judgment of so much guilt in the world begins with one's own relatively unimportant guilt, as if others weren't even guiltier and one were not oneself complicit in every other guilt—is not only sufficiently important; it is of fundamental importance: the unmasking of evil and its unacceptability for oneself, beginning with one's own evil. Isaiah's "Woe!" applies justifiably "to those who call evil good and good evil" (5:20). Only through one's own denunciation of evil—which also indirectly shows that the debt owed by this evil is the good—is it possible to stand firm against evil and guilt and to refuse to make any justifications either for one's own guilt and complicity or for the guilt of all the guilty. Guilt and complicity may well be what they are, but they nonetheless shouldn't exist, and one day, they no longer will!

10. The Unacceptable Contradiction

At first glance, this expectation of an ultimate triumph of the good may seem like a statement of faith and, judged disparagingly, like nothing but a statement of faith, whose coherence is based solely on revelation: the revelation of the—in the end—messianic good everywhere. Yet this "In the end only good!" also emerges as the final prospect of the knowable factuality of good and evil according to the standards of reason and science.

While the prospect of evil's one day becoming so powerful that it could bring about the downfall of all human beings presents—like the potential suicide of every individual—a real possibility, the following is however unthinkable: it is not possible to imagine how a living humankind could ever be exclusively evil. For its evil misses the mark of the good to the same extent to which it proves itself to be evil, thereby always also bearing witness to the good, if only as a good owed. But a humankind that would one day be exclusively good is, based on the factuality of good and evil, a possible, that is to say perfectly imaginable, prospect: Zephaniah's "You need not fear evil any more" (3:15).

The good and only the good is what evil never is: sufficient unto itself. Or the good is at the very worst not yet good enough, whereas evil is always guilt. This guilt points beyond its evil to the good, whereas the good only points to how this or that good deed ought to be amplified into an even better good and continue to proliferate in the form of this good. Evil lacks the good of which it falls short and is itself therefore merely something penultimate, and it would remain penultimate even if it were to ultimately become overpowering. Yet the good lacks nothing but its own consummation: in the end only good!

Chapter 11

CONTRADICTION SET FREE!

Dialogic instead of dialectics

Dialogic speaks of openness because it has the capacity to be open. It is not vexed by contradictory theses and antitheses, and it has no need of a synthesis that sublates them. For the openness of contradiction set free—a freedom that, at the height of its consummation, sets limits for itself, limits of and in freedom—in fact includes the entire All, whose modern completeness has blasted apart every monologic and mocks all dialectics, both of which want to reductively bring its diversity into line, as if all its beads could be strung on a single strand.

"And yet one must decide," interjects the dialectician, as if diversity precluded decisiveness. Dialogicians can respond that it is precisely they who decide and who, most importantly of all, stand by their decision, and in doing so demonstrate, in every essential respect, a much more unambiguous decisiveness than the dialectician ever can. For the latter remains faithful to his or her dialectics on the grounds of principle [*grundsätzlich*], which demands that he or she make shifting decisions, whereas the dialogician, whose dialogic only permits decisions on the grounds of acknowledging or establishing limits [*grenzsätzlich*], can thus remain faithful to him- or herself, unwavering in the face of all the shifts and vicissitudes he or she must also reckon with. One's opponent can contradict as assiduously as he or she likes! One's own foundation, to which one's opponent in this way sets limits, does not thereby lose its validity; its validity is rather reinforced by the fact that the other foundation, to which it likewise sets limits, is also justified.

The Whole of the dialectician's world breaks apart when his or her concluding synthesis is proven to be not as true in principle [*grundsätzlich*] as he or she had assumed, but the dialogician's world confirms that when two truths contradict each other, each is only true in a limited and limiting way [*grenzsätzlich*]: for it is only together that they constitute the Whole of truth.

In this way dialogic remains open even to dialectics, which it contradicts and which contradicts it, whereas dialectics goes off on yet another imperious rampage every time it encounters the contradiction of dialogic. Contradictions can, to the extent that the dialectician acknowledges them at all, present to him or her just one more antagonistic thesis or antithesis to be overcome as far as possible in the here and now, until it is—sooner or later—overcome completely, overpowered by the future synthesis. For the dialogician, however, the dialectic is and remains worth thinking through as a laudable progression to the complete apprehension of the historical diversity of contradiction and of every contradictoriness of the All. Yet dialectic should—and this is dialogic's only demand—dialectic should also stand by its own discovery! The dialectic comprehends far more than it admits to itself, for it still circles, after the fashion of antiquity and the Middle Ages, around a single center.

Whereas dialectics pushes dialogic aside—just like it ultimately pushes aside everything that bars the path of its own objective—dialogic includes dialectics the same way it includes, through to every end, everything that contradicts any of its standpoints. Yet there does exist one wrong that has no proper justification, the thoroughly "unacceptable contradiction" of evil! But it is precisely here that dialectics, because it knows nothing worthy of being negated absolutely, fails to recognize that evil is evil in all circumstances; that is to say, it fails to recognize any real evil at all. All claims made by the other are, insofar as they contradict the claim of dialectics, evil, but on the other hand they are never exclusively evil. For every contradiction constitutes a co-embodiment of the historical path to be traversed. In its historical moment—when the ascendant role falls to it—this contradiction is called good just as emphatically as it was once called evil and will afterward again be called evil, as soon as the moment allocated to it has passed. In this way, one can even hazard to take the side of the respective evil in order to, by fostering it, hasten the historical process by which it will ultimately be overcome. Taking the side of what is evil in the here and now—which is in truth not therefore any less evil—and reinforcing it serves, according to the dialectician, its increasingly undeniable unmasking and swifter overcoming, which is if nothing else a good cause.

For the dialogician, on the other hand—who observes the same development in which history, torn this way and that, is consummated, so that he or she also unreservedly affirms the dialectic, which grasps this process—the good remains good while evil remains evil: invariably and unmistakably! Under no circumstances does the cause sanctify the means, no matter how minor the evil of the means or exceptional the good of the cause. The decision for good or for evil, which in the case of dialogic is an utterly unambiguous decision, is not a decision between one side and another side that contradict each other; it is, rather, a decision that is made on both sides of their contradiction. It is a decision made at that point where each side must turn against [sich richten] its own evil in demonstration of its other truth, according to its own good!

Dialogic without dialogism

Just as the patience of dialogic is not negated by its intolerance towards evil, neither is its patience negated by its selectivity: its intolerance towards every form of dialogism. The four following dialogisms are to be rejected. Although they may appear to be shield bearers of dialogic, they are in fact and truth mere temptations that lead astray in the name of dialogic.

There is the danger, first of all, of overestimating the diversity of contradictions that must henceforth be sustained—as if on their account, unambiguity and resoluteness were things of the past. Second, there is the danger of overestimating the "Thou" as the model of entitlement to contradiction, empowering the "Thou" and only the "Thou" to direct the future, eventually decisive mode of interaction [*Miteinander*]. Third, there is the danger of pandialogism, an effect of overestimating the now standard paradigm of conversation [*Gespräch*]: trying to have a conversation everywhere and with everyone and everything. And finally, there is the danger of the literally irresponsible pluralogic: allowing oneself to be called into question simultaneously by any number of contradictions, instead of addressing the challenge posed by the one contradiction calling one to account in each respective case.

The overestimation of contradiction antagonizes all unambiguity and resoluteness to the end of wakening their conscience. But conscientiousness that aims only at contradictions is not capable of anything constructive; and when it comes to destruction, which is its primary aim, it is perhaps not ineffective, but nonetheless thoroughly fruitless. The battle against every one-sided claim to the whole truth, which in itself is justified and even necessary, is always a precursor of dialogic; but when an obsessive focus on contradictions exhausts itself in struggling against the hubristic claims of others, it is not even a precursor. The attempt to be the conscience of one's respective "Thou" or of any other at all is merely an evasion of one's own conscience and in fact unconscionable. The breakthrough to dialogic can only be accomplished from within one's own monologue. The only fruitful path is: to judge and right oneself [*richten*].

Overestimating the "Thou," on the other hand, means plunging into the humility of dependency in order to secure in one's other a once again independent master, whom one has, however, forced into this role, thereby setting oneself up as the surreptitious master of the master. Every express privileging of the "Thou" that stops at "I and Thou" without going beyond it to "Thou and Thou" remains imperiousness: a final act of egoistic hubris that must be dismantled, along the path of dialogic it initiated, for the sake of dialogic. One who confesses the slogan "I and Thou" claims unreserved responsibility for the "Thou," and yet the "Thou" of this "I and Thou" is also known, thought, felt, and directed by this confessor, who thereby distinguishes him- or herself as an I. The real "Thou," however, represents a contradiction, a contradiction that the other "I" that it calls to account—and which is therefore now a "Thou" in its own right—did not put into the other who is asking it this question. This contradiction leads to responsibilities that its "Thou," which can no longer be a mere I, may not have been aware of on its own, and may at first hardly understand, and may under some circumstances have little desire to hear, and even less desire to accept; but accept them it must.

Then there is the danger of pandialogism, according to which contradiction, which not only distinguishes and separates all the various elements that come together in its frame but also interconnects them, is supposed to foster a "conversation" everywhere and with everyone and everything, between "Thou" and "Thou." But the question of responsibility's challenging and its response, and the slogan "Contradiction Set Free," do not refer only to ways of speaking. They refer instead to a simile, and this simile's "dialogue" has at its disposal, for every possible mode of interaction, an exemplary counterpart [*Ent-„Sprechung"*] for all utterances, loud or quiet, as well as all nonverbal acts and omissions. Involvement and encounter do not require that everyone, at any time, be able to speak with everyone and everything, including works of art and animals, plants, mountains, clouds, and stars, talking and permitting oneself judgments about everyone and everything. Such a questioner of everyone and everything is in turn called into question by one and all: addressing everyone and everything as "thou" [*duzend*] and being addressed as "thou" [*geduzt*] by everyone and everything. A real conversation is only possible in an encounter between equals. Upholding the standard of dialogic in every instance does not mean everything should be brought into "conversation" with everything and everyone, without regard for one's own and others' dignity, level, rank, class, and respective task: without considering whether, or to what degree, a human being may be engrossed entirely by the demands of his or her task. Command and obedience, example and emulation, decree and implementation, direction and subordination preclude questions, and they only seem to involve answers: questionlessly calling into question, answering without being asked.

Finally there is, once flight into pandialogism has been blocked, the evasive maneuver of pluralogic. In reiterating the slogan "Thou and Thou," it endorses the slogan "Thou and Thou and Thou and Thou etc." in an attempt to simultaneously address a plurality of contradictions, whereby it merely abdicates its responsibility for the particular contradiction that calls it into question at any given time. Without surrendering oneself—and unreservedly surrendering oneself at that—there can be no encounter with the "Thou," which must in turn also surrender itself without reserve. During this mutual self-surrender, neither partner can simultaneously respond to any other "Thou," let alone to a plurality of them. To be sure, one is not called to account by only a single contradiction; one must respond to multiple contradictions and to as many of them as possible, to each as a questioning by a "Thou." This is why the recently popular podium discussions, for example, do not demonstrate dialogic, but rather almost always fall short of it. The inclusion of a plurality of contradictions in such conversations does more to prevent than to expand substantial discussion. A "Thou" must literally "address" its "Thou" in order to involve it, and it only really addresses and involves its "Thou" insofar as it can and does contradict it, whereby every other claim is drowned out. On the one hand, everyone has a claim to the answer of love, to "love your fellow as yourself" (Lev. 19:18), but on the other hand, this claim is only ever made by that self who is "nearest" one here and now. Even the question "And who is my neighbor?" (Luke 10:29) merely evades, by alluding to the plurality of possible others, one's respective neighbor—who of course can be every other human being without exception but is precisely not every other, but always that particular "nearest" human being who, prior to every question put to him or her, already calls the questioner into question.

Set contradiction free!

Freedom's imperative to set itself limits, insofar as it can do so in freedom and because of freedom, does not constitute an objection to freedom. It is precisely by doing so that it achieves consummation. And in the same way, dialogic demonstrates its openness by closing itself off again and again to merely alleged forms of openness or at least by distinguishing itself from those that are generally open, yet still far from being as literally cleared up [*aufgeräumt*][1] as dialogic itself is. Dialogic is neither convergence, competition, nor coexistence; it is not mere tolerance and not just cooperation; it is by no means collaboration, and it is something other than coordination, correlation, communication, and complementarity.

Although the "foreseeable meeting" of convergence, the gradual, mutual approach of contradictory paths to the same future goal, avoids that intolerance which in dialectics erupts with every step taken towards every other step, it nonetheless remains under the spell of this intolerance. Ultimately—namely in respect to the goal of the entire All—it insists on the possibility of anticipating an allegedly all-encompassing final synthesis. Apparently conciliatory to the extent that it recognizes an adversary that contradicts it, and in that sense akin to dialogic, on the other hand it is an imitation of dialectics and irreconcilably separated from dialogic by the deepest of abysses. It is a continuation of monologic rather than a demonstration of dialogic. In the contradictions convergence perceives, it sees and is only capable of seeing temporary obstacles along the path to a final unity, in whose name it "tolerates" the contradictions it tolerates only "along the way" while remaining certain of a coming sublation of its and all contradictoriness.

Compared to convergence, competition—this initially free "race" and ultimately free contest—is almost more honest. Competition permits the mutual contradiction of whatever is always mutually contradictory without taking one or the other side or setting itself any other goal than the possibility of every adversary being outdone by every other adversary. There is only one thing it prevents, and it does so only in order to keep competition truly open: the development of an excessive advantage by one of the competitors into a monopoly and its perpetuation. In just the same way, dialogic also fends off the monologue as soon as monologic attempts to overdevelop and perpetuate it. But competition does not take the contradictions between its competitors truly seriously. Discussions are not contests, encounters are not races, and struggling to mutually outdo one another is not a means of coming to terms with one's respective contradictions. The freedom established by competition is established thanks only to competition's aimlessness, such that the unfreedom that results from convergence's own objective would almost be preferable, if there wasn't also such a thing as real freedom.

And coexistence? The "existence together" of the different, the shared presence of what is contradictory: doesn't coexistence constitute the correct interpretation of what dialogic calls for, and what convergence and competition miss? This conjecture is wrong, and in fact no interpretation of dialogic deserves to be more trenchantly dismissed! Herbert Lüthy was correct to begin his francophone speech of 1962, "After the Cold War," with the following words:

> That the unspeakable word "coexistence" has become the consolation for our time characterizes the indigence of its hopes. Coexistence doesn't mean peace, but rather at most the consequence of the impossibility of peace as well as of the decision for war: the resigned, yet always only provisional parallel existence of the irreconcilable. Not without reason are the admonishers now ranging through the country preaching vigilance against the spiritual softening of an indolent peace [...] Neither the admonishers nor their warnings are ridiculous.[2]

For why does coexistence establish the shared existence of the different? Why does it let what is contradictory subsist together? Because according to coexistence, the moment does not yet seem to have arrived in which its own complete victory, with which it unswervingly and intolerantly reckons, can be achieved. And so it gains a respite—not a respite in which to better reflect on the possibilities of peace, however, but rather a respite in which it considers how to better attack its goal of completely eliminating every other that contradicts it. That is why coexistence permits the contradiction of its respective other: it is the last trump of the dialectic. Coexistence in this guise responds to all the demands of dialogic without departing from its own imperiousness. The diversity of contradictions that, with and because of the modern completeness of the world—and on the grounds of this completeness of the world—calls to account is always only apparently taken seriously by coexistence until the moment when it once again attempts to realize its own silently maintained objective through the totalitarian arrogation of totality—strengthened, so it reckons, by the respite. A delay, so the thinking goes, can only play into its own, that is, the inevitable future victor's hands.

So is it tolerance, "indulgence" that is called for? Who wouldn't want to answer in the affirmative, in view of the exemplary courage and thousandfold legitimacy of its demand, which is neither self-evident nor unhazardous, and which, in the struggle against every form of intolerance, is still anything but obsolete? And yet indulgence is not the same as dialogic, and dialogic is never mere indulgence. For what is at the back of tolerance is either an indulgence that is only provisional and merely puts off the victory on which it continues to insist or else the relinquishment of every ultimate objective whatsoever. In this way, past intolerance converts to a struggle against one's own and every intolerance, as if setting goals and striving towards victories were as such impermissible, and as if this relinquishment were a step forward, namely the step forward to dialogic. But indulgence is at best only a precondition of dialogic, which progresses by patience, and not a blindly indulgent patience, but a resolutely judicious one. The indulgence of tolerance thus, despite at first helping to blaze a trail to the openness of dialogic, ultimately misses the mark of dialogic, owing to the exclusivity of its demand for openness. And it is furthermore in no way up to the task of preventing its own abuse by the dialectic and the dialogisms. To merely be "decidedly" in favor of openness as such, and to therefore tolerate anything, is not enough. This decidedness must yet conceive of itself as a decision that need be ashamed neither of the goal nor of the victory of its dialogic but must rather assert them, follow through with them, and tenaciously defend them with the utmost strength and passion.

Openness for the sake of working together rather than openness as an end in itself: that is how dialogic defines the objective of its openness. Cooperation is welcome in this regard, although it advocates the right path in too lackluster a way; but most unwelcome is collaboration[3], in every manifestation a profoundly misguided aberration. Because cooperation for the most part only expresses good will, but without fully and explicitly committing to the seriousness and gravity of the will's testing, it must be deepened by that which the concept of dialogic announces with its conscious and express allusion to dialectics, which is thereby—consciously and expressly—shown its limits. Cooperation is therefore also dialogic, but dialogic that has not yet achieved complete resoluteness. Collaboration, however, is and always will be, according to the standards of dialogic and all other measures, an utterly condemnable form of "working together" by betraying one's self, and it is to be rejected without exception. This is the nasty taste which the initially also lackluster concept of "working together" has acquired, and which ought to be preserved, so that this potential perversion of cooperation can be univocally criticized. It makes no difference whether the self-betrayal of the collaborator is genuine or mere pretense, whether its aim is to put itself in the service of a greater power or to furtively manipulate its other. Both approaches squander the fruits that working together otherwise bears for all involved: heightened self-confidence, the satisfaction of proving oneself, and progressive self-realization.

Coordination, on the other hand, this "arranging together," is less prejudiced than convergence, more connecting than competition, and not a mere ruse like coexistence. It is more resolute than tolerance, and most importantly, it does not require self-betrayal by one or the other of the participants in collaboration; but on the other hand it is thoroughly unhistorical, deeply uninspired or, at the very least—in a pejorative sense—all too objective. It lacks the exciting challenge of going along [*Mitgehen*] with one's other as well as the grave, complicated concern one feels when one's other responds to one's going along with him or her, which, by calling all self-sufficiency into question, confirms one's own independence and its necessity.

Into the gaps left open by coordination steps correlation. This "reciprocity" has more élan and requires one go along with one's other in a more concerned way, by which it above all also underscores reciprocal complementarity. But correlation remains indifferent to the question of whether or not the others who mutually complement one another are equals. The dialectic and the dialogisms also posit reciprocities, and the reciprocities posited by communication and complementarity even retain much good; this good must, however, since the dawning of dialogic, be distinguished as less good as compared to the better good of dialogic in order to clear the way for this better good.

When it comes to indifference—at least ultimate indifference—communication must also be reproached. Like correlation, its "message" is either not at all or only marginally interested in the number, character, reciprocal relations, and ways of working together of its participants. Because communication requires an other in order to impart its message, it therefore seeks out encounters, requires encounters, in which it not only imparts its own messages but also—perhaps—receives them; and with that, communication's task is complete. It is only incidentally, and above all thanks to Jaspers, that communication also constitutes a philosophical concept. But it provides no basis for negating monologic or for drawing a contrast to the dialogisms. It supports neither a clear rejection of the dialectic's weaknesses nor an equally unambiguous retention of its essential achievements: central concerns of the concept of dialogic that are reflected even at the level of its verbal coining.

And, finally, complementarity, "completion through mutual exclusivity," is—like cooperation—not so much in need of being distinguished from dialogic as of being deepened by it. By, for example, acknowledging the reality of both space and time taken together—despite the impossibility of ever determining them simultaneously—complementarity demonstrates that the dialogical is a basic fact of the All. Dialogic, however, demonstrates that dialogue is a literally foundational, groundlaying task that always remains yet to be realized. The complementarity of the All persists whether it is recognized or not, whereas dialogic persists in the All only so long as its realization is ventured and succeeds. Complementarity is science and remains science; dialogic gives science an aim. The knowledge of dialogic, which is certainly also a form of research according to the standards of science, places one before opportunities that must yet be seized: through one's own actions! Complementarity thus anchors dialogic in universal laws, which, as such, still only make out the threshold of dialogic. With a foothold here, dialogic ventures and must venture a step further: from growth to maturity at the height of humanity's globally responsible consummation of freedom, whose terrifying splendor consists in the real possibility of its being bungled and perverted instead of realized.

Instead of sublation—Aufgeräumtheit

It is delightful, Hegel says in reference to the concept of sublation, which means "to preserve, to maintain, and equally [...] to cause to cease, to put an end to"[4]; it is a delight, Hegels says, "to find in the language words which have in themselves a speculative meaning; the German language has a number of such."[5] Another such word with a speculative meaning is the concept of *Aufgeräumtheit*, which only ever appears incidentally prior to its anchoring in dialogic, for example in Goethe:

Saint Peter wasn't *aufgeräumt*,
He'd just been dreaming while walking.

Sankt Peter war nicht aufgeräumt,
Er hatte so eben im Gehen geträumt.⁶

Sublation, Hegel goes on to say, this "fundamental determination which repeatedly occurs throughout the whole of philosophy"⁷ is in four different ways as much elimination as it is preservation, and at the same time it involves an upsurge, i.e., elevation into renewal. *Aufgeräumtheit* on the other hand, likewise a fundamental determination that reappears absolutely everywhere, is a threefold process of clearing-something-up [*Mit-Etwas-Aufräumen*], having-cleared-up [*Aufgeräumt-Haben*], and being-cleared-up [*Aufgeräumt-Sein*]. One who clears something up becomes, because he or she has cleared up, "cleared up" him- or herself: satisfied, well-balanced, cheerful, happy. The clearing-up one accomplishes outwardly becomes evident in oneself internally and externally according to the degree of one's success. By putting things in order, one puts oneself "in order."

The greatest satisfaction of *Aufgeräumtheit* is unavailable to sublation, whose eliminating, sublating mode of clearing-something-up clears its other out of the way, whereas *Aufgeräumtheit* clears up the fact that its other is standing in its way, or that something else, or it itself, is barring its other's way: putting every one, every other, and itself where they belong. The version of *having-cleared-up* that sublation initiates, in the form of what it calls "preservation," passes through the very real annihilation of its therefore henceforth merely "remembered" other, causing every possibility for an upsurge of joy to wilt and die—which the gloating dialectician, however, thanks to his Schadenfreude, doesn't miss. *Aufgeräumtheit*, however, has both the ability and the justification to rejoice in the full reality of the other involved in its *clearing-something-up*, thanks to the resulting real preservation of its other. The "sublation" undertaken by *Aufgeräumtheit* annihilates in the other, and with the other, only confusedness [*Unaufgeräumtheit*]: its own fault alone. Once overcome, neither it nor the All lacks anything whatsoever, for this is the only way that everything without exception comes into its own together and thus completely.

At sublation's peak, its dialectically achieved preservation and the skyward momentum of its uplifting renewal remain weighed down by the fact that they are inevitably a substitute for something whose sublation is the very act of its elimination. Only *Aufgeräumtheit*, which in this way once more brings to fruition a dormant potential of the dialectic that had been unable to mature within the dialectic itself, acknowledges everyone and everything in their respective areas of discretion, "eliminating" nothing but the failing of confusedness [*Unaufgeräumtheit*]. Dialogic itself can thus also, and rightly so, be *aufgeräumt*: itself full of joy in light of the joy it spreads.

Chapter 12

IN CONTRADICTION TO THE WORLD

The challenged environment

In addition to everything that has, up until our own time, called the human being and humanity into question and permitted the assumption that, to take responsibility for all that we are responsible for, we need but manage the diversity of contradictions, there is now a new challenge. The world, or—as seen from the perspective of the human being, which is also a world—that world which the human being is not, namely its environment, contradicts every attempt to establish oneself as its "lord and master." How speculative, how fatally naive this slogan suddenly sounds! With this slogan, Descartes had wanted to respond more adequately to the world than anyone ever had, and at first he did succeed in understanding the world better. But because he approached his other with the intention of controlling and owning it, his challenge ultimately fell short both of the world and of his own objective. What is done to the environment ultimately falls back on the world of the doer. Conversely, and for the same reason, one's world bears more bountiful and more substantial fruit when one proves oneself worthy of one's environment.

Descartes was nonetheless not wrong, or at least not completely wrong, to place his noteworthy first book *Discours de la Méthode* of 1637 above every form of speculation that was then being taught in the schools of philosophy. After a short period of reluctance, because Galileo had just—in 1633—been condemned for attempting the same revolution in thought, Descartes now addressed the public nonetheless, as he wrote, so as not to break the law "that obliges us to procure, as much as is in our power, the common good of all men." The former speculative philosophy should and can be replaced by a practical philosophy, which will allow us to know "the force and the actions of fire, water, air, the stars, the heavens, and all the other bodies that surround us, just as distinctly as we know the various skills of our craftsmen." Such that we, as Descartes jubilantly educes, might use our environment "in the same way, to use them for all purposes for which they are appropriate, and thus render ourselves, as it were, masters and possessors of nature."[1]

But nature contradicts. When challenged by humankind, nature confronts humankind—as its environment—with as much autonomy as only a human being can otherwise muster in resisting the human being.

Descartes was mistaken in wanting to use fire, water, air, the stars, the sky, and all the other bodies that surround us ("*qui nous environnent*") for all the purposes to which they are suited from a human perspective. But if humankind is to go beyond Descartes in the future, it must do so along the path he indicated, and to the end of a final progression to the same ultimate achievement. The challenge of an other that sets one limits is, as the end of the arbitrariness of one's own control and ownership, the beginning and the condition of a more fruitful way of working together—more fruitful also for oneself—with this other and with every other at the height of contradiction set free.

The Cartesian path on which we find ourselves, and which will eventually lead into the future, began millennia ago as cosmology, from whence it proceeded and inexorably proceeds to the further advances of theology and anthropology; whereby these three disciplines, like the terms "antiquity," "Middle Ages," and "modernity"—their respective "ages"—are again to be understood as ideal types.

The first, most extreme limit was encountered when the autonomous power of gods and humans, along with the "histories" to which they gave rise, stepped out of and confronted the world as it had been conceived by the doctrine of cosmology: as an unchanging domain, beyond the reach of human or divine intervention, of ultimate lawfulness and of the eternal necessity of unrelenting—and literally "unbeseechable"—adherence to the cycle of the All. For theology, and for every parallel medieval ideal type, this All becomes the historical creation of a single beginning leading to a single end. And for this history, which begins with the creation of the world and leads to its completion, the human being, created in the image of the creator, is—in opposition to the natural cycles to which history also gives rise—co-responsible.

Modern anthropology finally takes the complete responsibility of the human being, now fully conscious of its completeness, for humankind and for the All, as its point of departure—and at first did so as if there were no longer any cycles or at least none that could not be disregarded. But there are two different anthropologies. The human being of the first anthropology, which is actually only just emerging, is already conscious of its own responsibility and proceeds from this responsibility, presuming to do everything it can do and to exploit everything it can make use of. The human being of this anthropology takes the enduring authority of cosmology and theology for granted. They may manifest in an ultimate lawfulness on the one hand, or in an ultimate creative power on the other; either way, so this human being believes, they also protect those who set themselves up in their place as the lords and masters of creation. In the last analysis humankind remains, no matter what it perpetrates, safe from self-destruction, just as the All remains safe from the consequences of destruction at the hands of the human being.

There are thus also, as the human being of this first anthropology believes, "free commodities," an inexhaustible reservoir we owe to the providence of a loving "Mother Nature" or a loving "Father" of creation, which is ours to use, misuse, and even waste at will. And there is enough leeway to play around, as this line of thinking goes, a big enough margin for error for stupidity and malice! Like children and youths, the human beings of this first, early modern anthropology trust that no matter what they undertake—although they undertake it with all the power and force of adults—a lord of the world, or this world itself, will vouch for them when their recklessness goes awry. But such childlike trust is mere childishness in this hour of humanity's maturity.

By contrast, the second, but in fact first genuine anthropology conceives of itself as responsibility with no leeway for childish games, no guarantee against personal and universal downfall if human beings don't prevent their own self-destruction. This second anthropology, having been thought through to the end, also teaches that there has never anywhere been and never can be such a thing as "free commodities." Whatever a human being permits him- or herself in relation to matter and life—physically, mentally, or spiritually—he or she or someone else must sooner or later pay for one way or another, just as all human beings together must answer for everything that results from their recklessness, stupidity, and malice.

The henceforth pressing, total responsibility assumed by the human being who is fully conscious of his or her completeness at the height of the second, genuine anthropology, is responsibility vis-à-vis the All in the figure of the world as humanity and in the figure of this world as environment; an environment that contradicts humanity just as humanity contradicts it. The time for being the lord, for being the master, has passed. To be sure, medieval theology had placed such literally all-powerful omnipotence beyond the human being, in the hand of the creator. And when Turel, in his 1947 book *From Altamira to Bikini*, spoke of "Humanity as a System of Omnipotence" [*Menschheit als System der Allmacht*], it indeed seemed as if what his noteworthy book of 1931 had called the modern "Conquest of the Beyond" [*Eroberung des Jenseits*] had been ventured and accomplished.[2]

But only the first anthropology of the early modern period, to which in this regard even Turel remains attached, attributes omnipotence to humanity, because humanity had up to that point still attributed it to God. When the beyond is really conquered, it breaks apart in the here, setting limits to every here as an other here. The world as environment—which the human being, who is him- or herself also world, finds across from itself in the face of an All that has been rendered through and through "here"—now also sets limits, just as the human being sets limits for the human being on the grounds of modernity: the challenging, questioning limits of a contradiction. No matter whether it is the environment or another human being that contradicts: the other "here" of each appears in a beyond that is just as beyond as "the beyond" itself ever was.

These limits set by the challenge of a contradiction are not, however, just another impediment like the limits set by ancient cosmology, medieval theology, and early modern anthropology were, and for which reason they functioned as that seduction to speculation to which even Descartes succumbed. Even where no contradiction sets limits, an other is required: the other of speculative reality. It is something else entirely—that is to say, not speculation—to stop at the limits that a really contradicting other really sets. To observe these limits and thereby overcome expansion into the beyond in a completely responsible way, and in full consciousness of one's responsibility, by expanding in depth and deepening one's reach; this is, at this terminal point of all previous progress—which the challenged environment contradicts—precisely not the end of progress, but its consummation: maturity!

Challenging maturity

In the beginning there was growth; it lasted until modernity, at which point the complete encirclement of the earth and the complete encompassment of humanity presented limits that seemed to force a decision between growth and its renunciation. But this in no way means we have seen the end of growth, even if the unsustainable, haphazard mode of its continuation comes to an end. For the ending of this formerly "quantitative" growth also constitutes the beginning of "qualitative" growth's henceforth progressive deepening of growth, on one condition: the limits of previous growth—which call for its conclusion rather than for its continuation—must actually have reached the goal of really and permanently encircling the whole earth and encompassing the whole of humanity.

Adolescents, whose limits are still surmountable because they are still growing up, can only ever see the acceptance of limits as stagnation, as premature self-denial. That the acceptance of limits can lead to the conquest of a new threshold is something that neither childhood nor youth can ever grasp. But this is the only way a new path for progress can open up in an All that has come to encompass everything there is, should that indeed be the case. Instead of progressing in an old direction or yet another new direction, progress now becomes a deepening. If the goal until now had been to grow into new areas, transgressing limit after limit without being held accountable in any direction or for any area, the goal now, for one who has reached maturity in all directions and in all areas, is to prove oneself within the limits of one's All: responsible everywhere and always.

At the same time, maturity is also a new ability, but not just one more in the list of those one already possesses. This is because maturity delves into and grasps the now complete set of all one's abilities in a fundamentally new way. The mature grow, too, even though their expansion—which until now had been indistinguishable from growth—seems to have come to a standstill. Formerly it was the challenge of surmounting limits that led to further development, whereas now this function falls to the challenge of taking limits seriously. Consciously ceasing to expand when one has reached the merely apparent end of growth is in fact another step forward. It is precisely this step forward of deepening towards which growth itself grows, but for which it is not yet ripe so long as it insists upon expanding. The significance and renewed creative force of this step are evinced not least by a glimpse into a future committed to ecophilia, which will emerge as the fruit and consummation of the following prehistory.

Oikos, the Greek word for house, was combined with *nemo*, appropriate allocation, and *nomeus*, the good shepherd, to form *oikonomia*.[3] For inhabiting a place is more than merely settling; it is also the administration of households, the "economy" of the families, tribes, states, and gods. Zeus, too, the god of gods, is an *oikonomos*: father of the house and housekeeper in one. *Oikophilie*[4] thus already plays a role in Homer, where its meaning spans from taking care of one's house to loving one's home country—and this love of one's home country is enacted by looking after the household with concern for the inhabitants of all the country's homes, large and small, as well as the profitable development of its goods and the competent working of its lands.

In the same way, the biblical teaching of Jewry is likewise about land because it is about the welfare of the human being, and it always considers habitation with the entire household in mind. An arc stretches from the stranger, who is not to be oppressed—for "you know the feelings of the stranger, having yourselves been strangers in the land of Egypt" (Exod. 23:9)—to the poor among one's own people and the wild animals of the field, which are to be accounted for along with the land itself and its cultivation, including domestic animals and servants. "In just the same way"—as with the stranger, the poor, and the wild animal—"are you to preserve your vineyards and your olive groves. Six days you shall do your work, but on the seventh day you shall cease from labor, in order that your ox and your ass may rest, and that your bondman and the stranger may be refreshed" (23:9, 11–12).

Being free and being free to rest goes for the whole household, and not least for the ground that bears it. What human beings take from the land must—sooner or later—be replenished to the full extent of what was taken. If the land falls silent and the cities become desolate, as Buber's translation puts it, having been devastated and transformed by humankind into a desert (Lev. 26:33),

> then the land rests,
> it cashes in its rests.
> All the days of its silence it will rest,
> as it did not according to your customs of rest.
> (26:34, trans. after Buber)

All that belongs to the household is to be looked after for its own sake, so that all and everything flourish together. Just as no person may be constantly forced to serve, "the land must not be sold beyond reclaim" (25:23). The land, too, has a right to rest: the same right to freedom and the same right to restoration as animals and every person.

> But in the seventh year
> let there be rest, rest unto the land.
> (25:4, trans. after Buber)

This closedness of the ancient and medieval household was ruptured, however, and had to be ruptured. More comprehensively and, in every creative sense of growth, more consequentially fertile, was the household's division in the early modern period into economy, ecumene, and ecology. At the same time, economics [*Wirtschaft*] became the *Volks-Wirtschaft* of national economy, in opposition to the universalisms of ecumene and ecology, which claimed the whole of humanity and the whole earth as within their purview. Just as the state, science, art, and the personality of the human being as such had "emancipated" themselves, economics was now no longer the comprehensive *oikonomia* of Greek tradition and biblical teaching, but only economics in the sense of the profitability of every individual household: indifferent to every other household and to every other value.

This is precisely how the sixteenth century—which, in coining the term "economics," only apparently took up the Greek *oikonomia* of the whole household, but in fact only naturalized its own striving for profit—established the autonomy of humanity with its coining of "ecumene," instead of connecting humanity to the earth it inhabits in accord with the meaning of the original Greek. The concept of ecumene considers neither the economy nor the roots that bind human life to nature, from the water to the ground to the air and to light. Just as economics is ultimately concerned only with economic activity [*wirtschaften*] and no longer with the human being who performs it, ecumene thinks neither of the economy of human beings nor of ecology, because it is committed to the collectivity of human beings as such. The albeit sensible and necessary calls to ecumene were and are concerned almost exclusively with the mental and spiritual community of humanity, as if the mind and the soul did not reside in bodies that require a ground beneath their feet and were not, as living creatures, dependent upon their economy and upon the ongoing inhabitability of the earth upon which it is their wish and duty to be human.

Ecology, which finally pursues this root base of life, had only become self-conscious under this new name in 1873, and as a science it needed several decades more before it managed to include human life in the household of nature. Yet suddenly ecology has become a central, if not our exclusive concern, as if ecology's recognition as a university discipline meant the question of the environment—challenged to contradiction—had now been so thoroughly discussed that humanity and economics could be relieved of all further responsibility. At first, the belief that every other science and every other value were now superfluous was not unwelcome to ecologists, who profited from this overestimation of their science's potential. But what is now necessary, if only because the closed, holistic household of antiquity and the Middle Ages has irreparably broken apart, is not a specialized discipline, but an all-encompassing mode of research unconditionally open to every particular—and unconditionally open to every particular's right to distinguish its own particularity: ecophilia!

Ecophilia, which Homer had already tried to bring into circulation, evokes not only the development, but also the origin of that household of humanity and of the All it thinks together through to the end—and in so doing, this rarely ever used, in no way obsolete term offers itself as a slogan. It can accommodate the whole of the world, and along with this whole, everything that the love of house and home—which in the Greek and biblical contexts had already encompassed the whole of the household, yet in a largely undeveloped state—must come to encompass once again as a diversity that is henceforth full of contradictions, now that humanity has become the inhabitant of its household and begun to call the whole earth to account as its ground: humanity plus environment, this humanity's other.

In the 1960s, the concept of the "spaceship"—whose original ambition had been to expand the earth's reach—unexpectedly and encouragingly became an additional paradigm for the deepening of our range and scope on earth. "Spaceship thinking" [*Raumschiffdenken*], which joins ecophilia in announcing a new era, doesn't evoke what initially came to mind when humanity took its first steps towards space travel: the transgressing of limits. Rather, spaceship thinking evokes that which, once space travel had become a reality, quickly proved to be the essential and actual achievement of the "Conquest of the Beyond." From 1959 onward, the true lesson of space travel's achievement—irrevocably confirmed on April 12, 1961, by the first successful manned spaceflight—was the acceptance of limits!

Getting along with the given within one's limits, delving deeper into the respective range of one's respective spaceship, no matter what it reaches or doesn't reach on its flight—this is the actual, most difficult, and pathbreaking achievement. For their spaceship is all the space travelers have of the All and in the All. No matter how far their flight may take them, they can never fly beyond the limits of their own spaceship.

So, in the hour of ecophilia, the mastery of space travel—by which humanity had sought to grow beyond earth—has landed on earth and found its home. Having formerly only ever grown towards the All, at first childlike, then youthful humanity of antiquity and the Middle Ages has become the mature humanity of modernity. In mastering the spaceship, humanity becomes conscious of the mastery that will be demanded of it in the future. Humanity and humanity alone is fully responsible for all it has permitted itself in respect to the All.

Costs claimed

"Social costs"[5] is another key concept of the definitive anthropology and challenging future maturity of consummate modernity. With this new coinage, economics comes to the aid of ecology, and in so doing also comes to the aid of ecumene by admonishing and assisting it. Thanks to having thought "profitability" all the way through to the end, economics can now also help pave the way for ecophilia.

What are "social costs"? These are the costs that the economy passes along to society and its environment, the natural household of humanity. These are the costs that are not paid by the beneficiaries themselves, who are only interested in immediate profit, here and now. In service only to the competition of "profitability," the economies of both the West and the East have recklessly ignored, and continue to even more recklessly ignore, the destructive consequences of their production. That these "social costs" must be borne by others and by the All; that the settlement of their bitter and vicious account can only be deferred temporarily; that the economy itself ultimately remains in the reckoning: for a long time, as long as there were still open spaces and, above all, as many believed, "free commodities," all this went overlooked. Or perhaps it was understood once the finitude of the All and the interdependence of human beings and their economy with ecology made further avoidance of the accounting impossible, only to be repressed once again so that the growth of the economy could continue unchecked.

"As soon as one," K. William Kapp already wrote in 1950, in a critique directed, however—in exemplary self-critical fashion—almost exclusively against "The Social Costs of Private Enterprise," that ruthless exploitation perpetrated by private enterprise and the market economy, as if the planned state economy had any less reverence for the predatory plundering of resources:

> As soon as one passes beyond the traditional abstractions of cost-price analysis and begins to consider the omitted truth of social costs, it becomes clear once more that the alleged beneficial orderliness of the competitive process is all but a myth. For, if entrepreneurial costs do not measure the total costs of production, the competitive cost-price calculus is not merely meaningless but nothing more than an institutionalized cover under which it is possible for private enterprise to shift part of the costs to the shoulders of others and to practice a form of large-scale spoliation which transcends everything the early socialists had in mind when they spoke of the exploitation of man by man. [...] The first step toward a reorientation of economic science must be a return to philosophy.[6]

A return to philosophy, by which Kapp means overcoming the exclusive focus of economic thought by reconnecting it to ecology and ecumene, and thereby progressing towards the ecophilia of their contextualization within the contemporary and historical whole of the world of humanity and of the environment as the no less recklessly exploited household of nature. Such a return to philosophy can explain two things.

It is not profiting as such, but only such profiteering as has succumbed to the dictates of growth that shies away from no sacrifice in its service to—and idolatry of—the growth rate. This sacrifice, i.e., the destructive consequences recklessly taken into the bargain by the belief that supports such profiteering—faith in the higher meaning of growth as the only normative value—is not charged to its own account. The damage is borne by its victims. And while this economic mismanagement is nothing new, its repercussions—and this is something cataclysmically new—will weigh heavily in the future.

Thanks to the complete encirclement of the earth and the equally complete encompassment of this earth's humanity and its modern maturity, every attempt at passing along responsibility for damages incurred here runs up against limits. What is done is no longer, and never again will be, done merely to others. The respective expenses incurred or, as the language of technology refers to its consequences—"friction loss"—do not constitute a beyond of the profits raked in; they are a deed that haunts its perpetrator. Even the perpetrator must help pay off what he or she has "sacrificed" in the here of what will eventually emerge as his or her merely apparent profit. Sooner or later the hour of reckoning will strike!

On the grounds of modernity, every human being and the whole of humanity are together responsible for all the consequences of all their actions, past and future.

Still, this discovery of social costs—initially unconsciously, and later consciously deferred—is not a regression compared to earlier times, but a step forward. For it leads to this breakthrough: in the future, damages caused will have to be set off against the benefits. This is the beginning of the overcoming of the economic mismanagement of earlier times and of the present age, with all its "unheard-of human sacrifices" [*Menschenopfer unerhört!*], as Goethe's "Bride of Corinth" [*Braut von Korinth*] laments.[7] As modernity becomes conscious of the once powerlessly incurred human and environmental sacrifices—the social costs—the guilt of an ultimately suicidal debt-accumulation becomes visible, for which modernity itself is certainly also, and to a terrible degree, but not solely, at fault. Modernity must furthermore be credited with the realization that this guilt and debt-accumulation must and can be checked.

Nothing and no one may be "sacrificed"! Slavery has become unbearable, the devastation of war has become a by no means unavoidable catastrophe, and the health risks posed, for example, by sound, water, and air pollution come at a price that must be paid—and this for an economic growth that, given the circumstances, is no longer in any way "profitable." Furthermore, every exploitation of women by men, of children by adults, or of the aged by youth constitutes an unacceptable passing along of costs to the respectively weaker party, the same damnable predatory exploitation human beings are guilty of vis-à-vis nature, as if they wouldn't sooner or later have to account for all the costs of their economic activity.

Yet no matter how staggering this view of the social costs of the present and of all times may be, it is precisely this view that constitutes a turn towards better times in the future.

Every human being counts, and that means every human being without exception, of every age and of both sexes, weak and strong, sick and healthy; just as every human being of every skin color counts, and every human being of every faith and every knowledge! And just as every human being has its own dignity and value, so does the environment of the human being, from nature to culture, have its own dignity and—especially as nature—its own literally irreplaceable value. The question of whether the social costs can, in the future, be completely "internalized," such that profits would only then not be losses, and only then be justified, to the extent that the damages they unavoidably cause are included in the calculation of costs, and its victims are fully compensated; or whether these social costs will have to be at least partially assumed by society and thereby remain "externalized," is secondary. The revolutionary change remains in both cases the breakthrough to taking all social costs into account without exception.

From now on, only that counts as profit which is a profit in the face of reality in its entirety, which is to say, is not a merely apparent profit because the costs of its damage have been ignored. This is how we arrive, whereas until now only expansion mattered, at deepening. Not only the proceeds, but the damages, too, carry weight. From now on, the only growth that counts as growth is such that bears fruit in harmony with all that it consumes—and bears fruit also for those without whose seed it wouldn't be capable of bearing any fruit at all.

But while the concern of this transition from the previous standard of quantity to the solely justifiable future standard of quality of growth is indeed the future, it is not this future alone that is at stake. The other goal is to finally overcome the idolatry that is deeply rooted in the souls, minds, and economy of the present, an idolatry whose abandonment would result in the present—so this present believes—losing its true meaning.

Not only the followers of Adam Smith, but also those of Karl Marx find themselves called into question by this challenge. For both pioneers believed that growth in the external and outward senses of extension, expansion, and maximization of production and its "takings" constitutes the essence and proof of economic viability. Private enterprise and the market economy thus put their faith, when it comes to the domestic competition of capital, which of course also reaches beyond national borders, in growth and growth alone, while the Marxist command economy likewise reveres growth. The latter's concern is to outstrip capitalism through international competition. Setting limits to capitalism would mean the end of the freedom of the market, and soon every freedom, so the belief goes, would likewise come to an end. On the other hand, however, if the growth of the command economy were to be limited, Marxism would indeed forfeit the possibility of ever completely "overcoming" [*aufheben*] capitalism.

But is Marxism therefore already finished, if, and because, it turns out to be "merely" equal to its capitalist other? And does the market, on the other hand, cease to be an economy of competition if, and because, it is forced to take responsibility for the costs of its profits?

Contradiction set free, the freedom to engage in dialogic, arises here once again as the necessity of progressive *Aufgeräumtheit*. With the sole exception of the failure of confusedness [*Unaufgeräumtheit*], nothing whatsoever is to be eliminated; rather, each and all must be accorded their appropriate purview, on the respective grounds of which they can all bear fruit together in their mutually contradictory directions. The diversity of their contradictions is, if sustained rather than overcome [*aufgehoben*]—as if the latter were even possible—neither stagnation nor regression. It is, rather, progress: progress towards the prosperity and maturity of the completely developed wholeness of the modern All.

Both are necessary, although they contradict one another: the market economy and the planned economy, entrepreneurship and the state, just as the world of the human being and the world of the environment both are necessary, although they contradict each other. And economics and ecology are also both necessary, despite the contradiction between them. And facing them, contradicting them just as they contradict it, is ecumene, a further necessity. Economic viability is not wrong simply because holistic concern for the household is also right or because humanity is also in the right in trying to avoid becoming the economy's victim, despite nonetheless paying dearly for the upkeep of its household, perhaps even at great sacrifice.

The aim of this breakthrough—of from now on including all damages in accounting for the costs of use—is not to eradicate social costs, for without them there would be no human cultivation of the world, but to abolish the practice of passing them on to the victims. What is done must be answered for, and undertakings that result in the victim walking away uncompensated are impermissible.

But hasn't the hour of the "throw-away society" struck? Aren't we within reach of wealth to the point of excess, an incomparable prosperity that in the future—which will soon include all those who are still in need—will permit all human beings in the whole world without exception to do precisely that which, until now, was only permitted the few, and at the cost of others: to waste?

To be sure, the concept of the "throw-away society" also expresses a sort of accusation and ultimately even an unambiguous denunciation. At first, however, one discerns only what seems to be an essentially flattering charge, and one that is new to humanity: that its modernity has, or will soon have at its disposal, such abundant wealth that it can afford to waste it. Yet even when this reproach embedded in the concept of the "throw-away society" is heard, it is no match for the equally audible self-praise of wastefulness, which for thousands of years was the special privilege of gods, priests, and kings, while human beings looked on in amazement. Then as now, human beings had boundless admiration for wastefulness, because they themselves were at best just barely making do with what they had.

Although it is true that humanity's self-conception as a "throw-away society," its outward acceptance of the charge and inward acceptance of the flattery, constitutes the fulfillment of an ancient wish, the modern realization of this wish is not a continuation of the wastefulness of the prehistoric and historical past. The wastefulness of the past was—when, in the course of events, a small minority was indeed wasteful—for the most part an expression of humanity's immaturity. But at the height of humanity's maturity, only mere childishness still expresses itself that way. In this hour of the permanent and real encirclement of the whole earth and encompassment of the whole of humanity, all throwing away is, and can be only, a passing of the buck. It puts the burden of the costs of one's own wastefulness on other people or on the environment and thus victimizes them.

The so-called throw-away society is a society that passes the buck, nothing more. It has resulted and continues to result in nothing but debts for which others must answer. But those who have, while boasting of their squandering, simply passed the social costs on to others will also be required to pay in the end—not when they choose to do so, but in an unexpected and inconvenient hour of merciless reckoning.

Required: Human beings!

It is not to other humanities of other stars, which are mere excuses—just like the stores of resources supposedly waiting on other planets to replace the earth's depleted resources are mere excuses—that humanity addresses its "Thou," but to the environment with which it has collided and will continue to collide in increasingly contradictory ways in the future. Human beings' justifiably much-vaunted openness to the world [*Weltoffenheit*], their "eccentricity," which distinguishes them from the boundedness of "centered" animals whose environment is only ever a literally ineluctable world of their own: this worldly openness of human beings is not their ultimate end. Their ultimate end, after the penultimate stage of openness, begins when humanity experiences its contradiction of the world as a process of being called into question by the world and faces this questioning with autonomous responsibility towards it. The world, humanity's environment, with which humanity is not coextensive, holds, and is allowed to hold, the world of humanity responsible, as only a Thou can call another Thou into question in an encounter between equals.

In this way, that maturity which previously, so long as an immature humanity was still kept safely in the custody of its cosmology and theology, had only been attained and lived by individual human beings has now become the fate of humanity itself. In the hour of consummate modernity, its limits are not limits meant once more to be transgressed, meant to be accepted only provisionally until the further growth of one's childhood or one's youth again outgrows them. Rather, these limits, which are now the limits of a conscious anthropology, are insurmountable and must be accepted as permanent. It is precisely their permanent acceptance that opens up the further possibility and new creative challenge of "qualitative growth."

But that these limits of henceforth mature humanity are not just limits that it sets for itself, whereby it would just get stuck in a monologue or in dialectics, so in either event in a monologue: this is prevented by the environment as it takes its turn to speak in its own unmistakable way. It is what the dreamed of, hoped for and thousands upon thousands of times imagined other humanities, which are nothing but excuses, are not: a real other that physically contradicts humanity. It is the environment that presents humanity—at the height of "dialogic without dialogisms"—with responsibilities of which humanity on its own may not have been aware, and which it may at first hardly understand and possibly be reluctant to hear, yet which it must, though even more reluctantly, nonetheless accept.

But the suggestion that humanity's maturity means that it is now superfluous for individuals themselves to be mature is just another of their excuses. Humanity's own maturity does not suffice to confer maturity upon its individual members. Yet the modern individual, on the presumption that it can leave its responsibility to humanity as such, takes much greater liberties with its immaturity than human beings of earlier ages ever dared.

Never before has childhood been so extensively savored as it is now, on the grounds of modernity, especially since the transition to humanity's maturity, which has now become conscious, brings with it conscious awareness of the other periods of life going all the way back to prenatal existence. The meaning and fundamentally autonomous uniqueness of the nine months following conception, and of the early life of the newly born human, have only been clear for a few decades. And never before has youth, as a period of life subsequent to early childhood and childhood, enjoyed itself so carelessly—and rightly so. This is because maturity—and the maturity of humanity, before the background of which the other periods of life have now "emancipated" themselves—is, in contrast to the respective progressions of each of these periods of life with their respective sublations [*Aufhebung*] of all the steps leading up to them, the fundamentally different progression of *Aufgeräumtheit*, which acknowledges all the steps together: dialogic realized.

So long as quantitative growth was paramount, that which is henceforth unavoidable at the level of qualitative growth, and in this hour of maturity, was not yet even possible. The mutually contradictory aspects of every period of life and of everything whatsoever can and ought to be acknowledged all together!

On the other hand, humanity exists only in the form of the individuals that make it up. That and only that which begins with them has truly begun. If every single human being does not achieve his or her own maturity, humanity is, despite its own maturity as such, nonetheless lost. The goal of humanity can only be reached when every human being reaches it, and that means every single one without exception!

Individuals cannot and may not rest content with the fact that humanity as such has grown into the responsibility that all see before themselves as their own individual goal; nor can they rest content that they themselves face this responsibility. Meaning and fruitfulness and joy, freedom and peace, are either secured for all or certain for none. The possibility we now have of embracing the proper autonomy of every period of life in a way that enables each to flourish in the fecundity of its own age, either completely, or at least insofar as it does not prevent another stage of life from fulfilling its own potential, is founded on the following condition: it must also be possible, everywhere in the whole world, for that period of life to prove itself in which personal maturity is capable of taking responsibility for guaranteeing the continued existence, here and now and in the future, of dignified human life and of an environment together with which this life can bear fruit here, now, and in the future.

In view of humanity's maturity, it is more important than ever before that human beings become mature human beings. For it is up to every individual human being that makes up this humanity—and to nothing and to no one else besides—to ensure that their world and the environment it faces do not perish, but endure.

NOTES

Introduction

1. Chapter 1, 17.
2. Theodor W. Adorno, *Negative Dialectics*, trans. E. B. Ashton (New York and London: Continuum, 2005), 3. The opening line of *Negative Dialectics*.
3. Hermann Levin Goldschmidt, *Der Nihilismus im Licht einer kritischen Philosophie*, in Goldschmidt, *Philosophie als Dialogik: Frühe Schriften*, vol. 1 (Vienna: Passagen, 1992), 19–100.
4. Hermann Levin Goldschmidt, *Philosophie als Dialogik*, in Goldschmidt, *Philosophie als Dialogik: Frühe Schriften*, vol. 1, 163–282.
5. Goldschmidt, *Werke*, vol. 1, 165–168.
6. Ibid., 168.
7. Ibid., 192f.
8. For a more detailed discussion of this point, see Willi Goetschel, "From Difference to Alterity: 'And' in Rosenzweig and Goldschmidt" in *Archivio di Filosofia/Archives of Philosophy* 86 (2018): 233–243.
9. Martin Buber, "Distance and Relation" in Buber, *On Intersubjectivity and Cultural Creativity*, ed. S. N. Eisenstadt (Chicago and London: University of Chicago Press, 1992), 57–67.
10. Hermann Levin Goldschmidt, *The Legacy of German Jewry*, trans. David Suchoff (New York: Fordham University Press, 2007).
11. Jacques Derrida, "Abraham, the Other" in *Judeities: Questions for Jacques Derrida*, trans. Bettina Bergo and Michael B. Smith, ed. Bettina Bergo, Joseph Cohen, and Raphael Zagury-Orly (New York: Fordham University Press, 2007), 1–35.
12. Moses Mendelssohn, *On the Evidence in Metaphysical Sciences* in Mendelssohn, *Philosophical Writings*, trans. Daniel O. Dahlstrom (Cambridge: Cambridge University Press, 1997), 251–306, 278.
13. Martin Buber, "The History of the Dialogical Principle" in Buber, *Between Man and Man* (New York: Macmillan, 1965 and 1985), 209–224.
14. Chapter 3, 31.
15. Chapter 3, 32.
16. Chapter 11, 117.
17. Leo Tolstoy, *The Complete Works*, vol. 24: *Latest Works, Life General Index, Bibliography*, ed. and trans. Leo Wiener (London: J. M. Dent & Co., 1905), 129–169, 132.
18. Pierre-Joseph Proudhon, *Les confessions d'un révolutionnaire pour servir à l'histoire de la Révolution de février* (Paris: Garnier, 1850), 323. See *The Making of the Modern World*, http://tinyurl.galegroup.com/tinyurl/6pqU67. Accessed August 3, 2018.
19. Chapter 7, 83.
20. Ibid.
21. Chapter 8, 93.
22. Chapter 5, 56.
23. Chapter 6, 59.

24 Chapter 12, 127.
25 Chapter 12, 137–38.
26 Chapter 12, 138.
27 Chapter 12, 139.

Chapter 1

1   Cf. Josephus, *The Life. Against Apion*, trans. H. St. J. Thackeray, Loeb Classical Library 186 (Cambridge, MA: Harvard University Press, 1926), *Against Apion*, 1: 22, 237. [Here I have translated Goldschmidt's German source directly. Trans.]
2   Plato, *Apology*, St. 20ff.
3   Plato, *The Republic*, trans. G. M. A. Grube (Indianapolis: Hackett, 1974), book 7, St. 533, 185.
4   Ibid., 184f.
5   Plato, Philebus in Plato, *Statesman. Philebus. Ion*, trans. Harold North Fowler and W. R. M. Lamb, Loeb Classical Library 164 (Cambridge, MA: Harvard University Press, 1925), St 16–17, 219–221.
6   Plato, *Republic*, book 7, St. 539, 189.

Chapter 2

1   Hermann Levin Goldschmidt, "Die Frage des Mitmenschen und des Mitvolks," in Goldschmidt, *Aus den Quellen des Judentums: Aufsätze zur Philosophie*, Werke, vol. 5 (Vienna: Passagen, 2000), 125–144, 127f.
2   See Longfellow's translation: "But now was turning my desire and will / Even as the wheel that is equally moved, / The Love which moves the sun and the other stars." Dante Alighieri, *The Divine Comedy*, trans. Henry Wadsworth Longfellow (London: Routledge, 1900), 148.
3   Peter Wust, *Gesammelte Werke*, ed. Wilhelm Vernekohl (Münster: Regensberg, 1963), vol. 3:2, 338.
4   Ibid., 397f.
5   St. Augustine, *City of God*, trans. Henry Bettenson (London: Penguin, 1984), book XI, chapter 18, 449.
6   Nicholas of Cusa, "On [Intellectual] Eyeglasses (De Beryllo)," § 32, in *Cusa, Metaphysical Speculations, Six Latin Texts*, trans. Jasper Hopkins (Minneapolis: The Arthur J. Banning Press, 1998), 792–838, 806.
7   Ibid., § 66, 824, trans. slightly modified with reference to Nicolai de Cusa, *Opera Omnia*, vol. XI/I: De beryllo. Ediderunt: I. G. Senger/C. Bormann, Hamburg 1988. Digital edition by Burkhard Mojsisch, 2008. https://www.hs-augsburg.de/~harsch/Chronologia/Lspost15/Cusa/cus_bery.html, accessed December 5, 2015.

Chapter 3

1   Johann Wolfgang von Goethe, *Faust: A Tragedy*, trans. Walter Arndt, ed. Cyrus Hamlin (New York and London: Norton, 2nd ed. 2000), *Faust*, part II, act 2, verses 6785–6789, 192.

2   Aristotle, Metaphysics, IV, 3. Cf. Hermann Levin Goldschmidt, *Philosophie als Dialogik*, in Goldschmidt, Werke, vol. 1, 192f. and "Philosophie als Dialogik," in Goldschmidt, Werke, vol. 5, 106f.
3   Franz von Baader, *Fermenta Cognitionis*, I, Preface, in von Baader, *Sämmtliche Werke*, vol. 2 (Leipzig: Bethmann, 1851), 141.
4   The Hegelian term *Aufhebung* denotes the final outcome of the dialectic, in which contradiction has been "overcome" or defeated by the onward march of history and its internal logic and contradiction's challenge has been "suspended" in Ideality. Depending on emphasis, *Aufhebung* can be translated as "overcoming," "suspension" or, more technically, "sublation." *Aufhebung* is the key Hegelian concept in dialogue with which Goldschmidt develops the counterconcept of *Aufgeräumtheit* (see Chapter 11). [Trans.]
5   Arthur Schopenhauer, *The World as Will and Presentation*, trans. Richard E. Aquila in collaboration with David Carus (New York: Pearson Longman, 2008–2011), vol. 2, §41.533.
6   Georg Wilhelm Friedrich Hegel, *Berliner Schriften (1818–1831)*, ed. Walter Jaeschke (Hamburg: Meiner, 1997), 43–61, 49.
7   *Hegel's Aesthetics: Lectures on Fine Art*, ed. Thomas Knox (Oxford: Oxford University Press, 1975), vol. 2, 668.
8   Georg Friedrich Wilhelm Hegel, *The Philosophy of History*, trans. J. Sibree (New York: Colonial Press, 1900), 19.
9   Karl Marx, *Capital, volume 1*, afterword to the second edition 1873, in *The Marx-Engels Reader*, ed. Robert C. Tucker (New York and London: Norton, 2nd ed. 1978), 299–302, 301.
10 Ibid., 302.
11 Mao, "On Contradiction," in Mao, *On Practice and Contradiction* (London and New York: Verso, 2017), 67–102, 72.
12 Ibid., 76.
13 Ibid., 79.
14 Ibid., 80.
15 Ibid.
16 Ibid., 67.
17 Ibid., 72.
18 Mao, "On Practice: On the Relation between Knowledge and Practice, between Knowing and Doing," in Mao, *On Practice and Contradiction*, 52–66, 65f.
19 Ibid., 91.
20 Ibid., 88.
21 Ibid.
22 Bertolt Brecht, *Journals 1934–1955*, trans. Hugh Rorrison, ed. John Willett (New York: Routledge, 1993), 384.
23 Martin Heidegger, "Zeichen," in *Neue Zürcher Zeitung* no. 579, September 21, 1969, now in Heidegger, *Aus der Erfahrung des Denkens, Gesamtausgabe*, vol.13 (Frankfurt a.M.: Klostermann), 211–212.
24 Ibid., 212.
25 Ibid.
26 Ibid.
27 Ibid. [Goldschmidt has inverted the order of the two parts of the quote. Trans.]

Chapter 4

1. Vladimir Ilyich Lenin, "Speech Delivered to the Moscow Gubernia Conference of the R.C.P.(B.)" in Lenin, *Collected Works*, 4th English Edition (Moscow: Progress Publishers, 1965), vol. 31, 408–426, 419.
2. Theodor Herzl, *The Jewish State*, trans. Henk Overberg (Jerusalem: Aronson, 1997), 129.
3. *The Complete Diaries of Theodor Herzl*, ed. Raphael Patai and Harry Zohn (New York and London: Herzl Press and Yoseloff, 1960), entry on November 7, 1895, vol. 1, 267.
4. Sigmund Freud, *Civilization and Its Discontents* (1930) in *The Standard Edition of the Complete Psychological Works of Sigmund Freud, Volume XXI (1927–1931): The Future of an Illusion, Civilization and Its Discontents, and Other Works*, 57–146, 90f.
5. Ibid., end of section VIII.
6. Hermann Levin Goldschmidt, *Weil wir Brüder sind: Jüdische Schriften 1935–1998*, Werke, vol. 9 (Passagen: Vienna, 2014), 89–99.
7. Adrien Turel, *Und nichts fiel auf ein gut Land* (Zurich: Turel, 1958), 363 and Turel, *Splitter* (1961), 23.
8. Adrien Turel, *Generalangriff auf die Persönlichkeit und dessen Abwehr* (Zurich: Turel, 1955), 2.
9. Goethe, "Der Zauberlehrling," in Goethe, *Sämtliche Werke*, ed. Ernst Beutler (Zurich: Artemis, 1950), vol. 1, 149.
10. Ibid., 152.
11. Ibid.
12. Freud, *Civilization and Its Discontents*, 90f.

Chapter 5

1. Karl Marx, *The Eighteenth Brumaire of Louis Bonaparte*, trans. Daniel De Leon (New York: The International Publishing Co.), 76.
2. Ernst Bloch, *Heritage of Our Times*, trans. Neville and Stephen Plaice (Berkeley and Los Angeles: University of California Press, 1990), 62.
3. Ibid., 97.
4. Ibid.
5. Ibid., 108.
6. Ibid.
7. Ibid.
8. Ibid.
9. Ibid.
10. Ibid., 113.
11. Ibid., 109.
12. Ibid., 110.
13. Ibid., 6.
14. Johann Christoph Friedrich von Schiller, *Wilhelm Tell*, trans. William F. Mainland (Chicago and London: University of Chicago Press, 1972), 55.
15. Ibid.

16 Ibid., 56.
17 Ibid., 55.
18 Theodor W. Adorno, "Erziehung zur Mündigkeit," in Adorno, *Erziehung zur Mündigkeit: Vorträge und Gespräche mit Hellmut Becker 1959-1969*, ed. Gerd Kadelbach (Frankfurt a.M.: Suhrkamp, 1970), 133–147, 145. [The English translation Theodor Adorno W. Adorno and Hellmut Becker, "Education for Maturity and Responsibility," trans. Robert French, Jem Thomas and Dorothee Weymann in *History of the Human Sciences* 12 (1999): 21–34, 30f has been modified. Trans.]

Chapter 6

1 Herbert Marcuse, *One-dimensional Man: Studies in the Ideology of Advanced Industrial Society* (Boston: Beacon Press, 1964), 250f.
2 Ibid., 255.
3 Hermann Levin Goldschmidt, "Schuld in der Sicht des Judentums," in Goldschmidt, *"Der Rest bleibt": Aufsätze zum Judentum, Werke*, vol. 4 (Vienna: Passagen, 1997), 47–64.
4 Robert Jungk, *Tomorrow Is Already Here*, trans. Marguerite Waldman (New York: Simon & Schuster, 1954).
5 Adolf Portmann, *Manipulation des Menschen als Schicksal und Bedrohung* (Zurich: Arche, 1969), 45.
6 Ibid., 46.
7 Adrien Turel, *Von Altamira bis Bikini, die Menschheit als System der Allmacht* (Zurich: Stampfenbach, 1947), 91.
8 Turel, *Generalangriff auf die Persönlichkeit und dessen Abwehr*, 61.
9 Hans Albert, *Treatise on Critical Reason*, trans. Mary Varney Rorty (Princeton: Princeton University Press, 1985), 56.
10 Ibid.
11 Karl Popper, *The Logic of Scientific Discovery* (London and New York: Routledge, 2002), 72.
12 Albert, *Treatise on Critical Reason*, 56.
13 Hermann Levin Goldschmidt, "Die Sackgasse de Nihilismus," in Goldschmidt, *Dialogik: Philosophie auf dem Boden der Neuzeit* (Frankfurt a.M.: Europäische Verlagsanstalt, 1964), 97–112.
14 Friedrich Nietzsche, *The Will to Power*, trans. Walter Kaufmann and R. J. Hollingdale (New York: Vintage, 1968), 3.
15 Hermann Levin Goldschmidt, "Der Nihilismus im Licht einer kritischen Philosophie," in Goldschmidt, *Werke*, vol. 1, 19–100.
16 Nietzsche, *Will to Power*, 18, §24.
17 Ibid., 69, §112.
18 Ibid., 19, §28.
19 Ibid., 18, §23.

Chapter 7

1 Leo Tolstoy, "Appeal to the Working People," in Tolstoy, *The Complete Works, vol. 24: Latest Works, Life General Index, Bibliography*, ed. and trans. Leo Wiener (London: J. M. Dent & Co., 1905), 150–152.

2   Ibid., 132.
3   Derrick Leon, *Tolstoy: His Life and Work* (London: Routledge, 2015), 79f., cited from *Tolstoy's Diaries 1853–1857*, trans. Louise and Aylmer Maude, ed. Aylmer Maude (London: Heinemann, 1927).
4   Max Stirner, *The Ego and His Own: The Case of the Individual against Authority*, trans. Steven T. Byington (New York: Dover, 2005), 223.
5   Proudhon, *Les confessions d'un révolutionnaire pour servir à l'histoire de la Révolution de février*, 217. See *The Making of the Modern World*, http://tinyurl.galegroup.com/tinyurl/6pqU67. Accessed August 3, 2018.
6   Ibid., 217f.
7   Ibid., 220.
8   Ibid., 323.
9   Stirner, *The Ego and His Own*, 223.
10 Ibid.
11 Ibid.
12 Ibid., 235.
13 Ibid., 223.
14 Ibid., 224.
15 Ibid., 235f.
16 Ibid., 260.
17 Michael Bakunin, "State and Society," in Bakunin, *Selected Writings*, ed. Arthur Lehning, trans. Steven Cox and Oliver Stevens (New York: Grove, 1974), 136–154, 151. [Goldschmidt follows Michael Bakunin, *Gott und der Staat*, in Bakunin, *Gesammelte Werke*, vol. 1 (Berlin: Der Syndikalist, 1921), 94–200, 182f. Trans.]
18 Ibid.
19 Bakunin, "State and Society," 151f.
20 Peter Kropotkin, *Words of a Rebel*, trans. George Woodcock (Montréal and New York: Black Rose, 1992), 167.
21 James Joll, *The Anarchists* (London: Eyre & Spottiswoode, 1964), 223.
22 Marcuse, *One-dimensional Man*, 256.
23 Ibid., 257.
24 Karl Marx, *The Communist Manifesto*, in Marx, *Selected Writings*, ed. Lawrence H. Simon (Indianapolis: Hackett, 1994), 167.
25 Michael Bakunin, *Statism and Anarchy*, trans. and ed. Marshall S. Shatz (Cambridge: Cambridge University Press, 1990), 7.
26 Marcuse, *One-dimensional Man*, 256.

Chapter 8

1   See Kurt Goldammer, *Der Mythus von Ost und West: Eine kultur- und religionsgeschichtliche Betrachtung* (Munich: Reinhardt, 1962).
2   Aristotle, *Politics: Books I and II*, trans. Trevor J. Saunders (Oxford: Clarendon, 1995), 1:4, 5.
3   Ibid.
4   Ibid., 1:5, 7.
5   Johann Wolfgang Goethe, "Natur und Kunst," in Goethe, *Sämtliche Werke*, vol. 2, 141.

6   Friedrich Wilhelm Nietzsche, *Thus Spoke Zarathustra*, ed. Adrian Del Caro and Robert B. Pippin, trans. Adrian Del Caro, Cambridge Texts in the History of Philosophy (Cambridge: Cambridge University Press, 2006), 46.
7   Friedrich Schiller, "Die Worte des Glaubens," in Schiller, Sämtliche *Werke, Säkularausgabe*, ed. Eduard von der Hellen (Stuttgart: Cotta 1904), vol. 1, 163f.

Chapter 9

1   Jacob and Wilhelm Grimm, "Death's Messengers," in *Grimm's Household Tales*, trans. Margaret Hunt (London: George Bell and Sons, 1884), vol. 2, 277–278, 278.
2   Ibid.
3   Plato, Republic, book 3, St. 407, 76.
4   For a critique of the World Health Organization's definition of health, see Hermann Levin Goldschmidt, "Natürliche—Unnatürliche Gesundheit" and "Natürliche und Unnatürliche Gesundheit," in Goldschmidt, *Haltet euch an Worte: im ganzen! Texte und Thesen*, vol. 7 (Vienna: Passagen, 2013), 197–204, esp. 198–200 and 209–214.
5   Giambattista Vico, *New Science*, trans. David Marsh (London: Penguin, 2000), 120.
6   Martin Heidegger, "Anaximander's Saying," in Heidegger, *Off the Beaten Track*, ed. and trans. Julian Young and Kenneth Haynes (Cambridge: Cambridge University Press, 2002), 242–281, 242. The rendering of Anaximander's saying is Goldschmidt's.
7   Hermann Levin Goldschmidt, "Kranke Leben auch," in Goldschmidt, vol. 7, 205–208, see also "Natürliche—Unnatürliche Gesundheit," 197–204, and "Natürliche und Unnatürliche Gesundheit," 209–214.
8   Max Scheler, *Man's Place in Nature*, trans. Hans Meyerhoff (Boston: Beacon Press 1961), 54.
9   Ibid., 55.
10 Heidegger, "Anaximander's Saying," 242.
11 Hermann Levin Goldschmidt, "Qualitatives Wachstum: Slogan? Mythos? Chance?" in Goldschmidt, *Werke*, vol. 7, 245–266.
12 Hermann Levin Goldschmidt, in "The Philosophy of Society", lecture Volkshochschule Zurich, January 17, 1974.

Chapter 10

1   Spinoza, *Ethics* in *The Collected Works of Spinoza*, ed. and trans. Edwin Curley (Princeton: Princeton University Press, 1985), 616.
2   Hermann Levin Goldschmidt, "Schuld in der Sicht des Judentums," in Goldschmidt, *Werke*, vol. 4, 47–64.
3   Hermann Cohen, *Religion of Reason out of the Sources of Judaism*, trans. Simon Kaplan (New York: Ungar, 1972), 183.
4   Goldschmidt, "Schuld in der Sicht des Judentums," in Goldschmidt, "*Der Rest bleibt*": *Aufsätze zum Judentum*, Werke, vol. 4, 47–64. See Mishna, Yoma 85b.
5   Hermann Levin Goldschmidt, *Weil wir Brüder sind* in Goldschmidt, *Werke*, vol. 9, 137f.

Chapter 11

1. See section 4 for an explanation of the terms *aufgeräumt/Aufgeräumtheit*.
2. Herbert Lüthy, *Nach dem Untergang des Abendlandes* (Cologne: Kiepenheuer & Witsch, 1964), 404.
3. "Kollaboration" in German is indelibly marked by the context of war and in Goldschmidt's usage carries the connotation of betrayal [Trans.]
4. Hegel, *Science of Logic*, trans. A. V. Miller (London: Allen & Unwin and New York: Humanities Press, 1976), 107.
5. Ibid.
6. Johann Wolfgang Goethe, "Legende," in Goethe, *Sämtliche Werke*, vol. 2, 108–110, 109.
7. Hegel, *Science of Logic*, ibid.

Chapter 12

1. René Descartes, *Discourse on Method and Meditations on First Philosophy*, trans. Donald A. Cress (Indianapolis and Cambridge: Hackett, 4th ed. 1998), 35.
2. Adrien Turel, *Die Eroberung des Jenseits* (Berlin: Rowohlt, 1931) and Turel, *Von Altamira bis Bikini*.
3. Ferdinand Wagner, *Das Bild der frühen Ökonomie* (Salzburg: Stifterbibliothek, 1958).
4. Homer, *Odyssey*, XIV, 223.
5. K. William Kapp, *The Social Costs of Private Enterprise* (New York: Schocken, first Schocken Edition, 2 ed. 1971), 13.
6. Ibid., 233 and 244.
7. Goethe, "Die Brauth von Korinth," in Goethe, *Sämtliche Werke*, vol. 1, 154.

INDEX

Abbahu (Rabbi) 113
Abel 21, 22
Abraham 22, 102
Adam 21, 22, 42
Adorno, Theodor W. 2, 3, 5, 9, 13, 56
Alaric I 27
Albert, Hans 67
Alexander the Great 18
Amnon (son of David) 96
anarchism 11–12, 71, 73–83
Anaximander 101
Apion 141
Aristotle 18, 32, 86, 87
Asclepius 95
Aufgeräumtheit viii, 121, 124–5, 136, 139, 142, 147
Augustine of Hippo 27, 28, 30

Baader, Franz von 33
Bakunin, Mikhail 73, 74, 75, 78, 79, 80, 81, 82
Becker, Hellmut 56
Ben Sira (Yeshua Ben Sirach) 28
Bloch, Ernst 54
Brecht, Bertolt 39
Buber, Martin 2, 3, 4, 5, 8, 9, 21, 87, 131

Cain 21, 22, 107
Cohen, Hermann 3, 4, 5, 8, 9, 111
Columbus, Christopher 49
cosmology 128, 129, 138
Courbet, Gustave 76

Dante Alighieri 26
Darwin, Charles 108
David (King of Israel) 96, 102
death 14, 95–106
Descartes, René 127, 128, 129
dialectic viii, 2, 4, 5, 8, 10, 13, 14, 19, 22–7, 33–41, 67–8, 117–18, 121–5, 138, 142

dialogic 1–10, 13, 15, 28, 40, 117–25, 136, 138–9
Diels, Hermann 101
Dollo, Louis 43

ecology 131–6
economy 5, 14, 41, 46, 47, 51, 52, 60, 62, 70, 109, 131–6
ecumene 131–6
Einstein, Albert 108
Either-And-Or 9, 10, 14, 31, 32, 36, 89, 91
emancipation 4, 13, 16, 59, 60, 87
Engels, Friedrich 36, 82
environment 127, 129–39
Eve 21, 22
evil 21, 27, 28, 31–32, 51, 75, 78, 98, 103–4, 107–15, 118
existentialism 35–6
Ezekiel 111, 113

faith 5, 17–18, 20, 22, 23, 25, 28–9, 34, 39, 50, 51, 68–9, 100, 115, 135
fascism 13, 41, 53–7, 59–60
Flechtheim, Ossip K. 63
freedom 9, 11–14, 41–8, 59–68, 69, 73–83, 85–94, 121
Freud, Sigmund 42, 43, 45, 81, 108
futurology 13, 41, 53, 62–6

Galileo Galilei 127
Gandhi, Mahatma 74
Godwin, William 11, 73, 77
Goethe, Johann Wolfgang 13, 32, 46, 47, 89, 124, 135
good 21, 27–8, 31–2, 42, 60, 66, 98, 103–4, 107–15, 118, 123
Grimm, Jacob 95
Grimm, Wilhelm 95
guilt 21, 43, 61, 64, 67, 74, 79, 98, 104, 107–15, 135

Index

health 14, 95–9, 102–6
Hegel, Georg Wilhelm Friedrich viii, 4, 9, 13, 22–4, 33, 34–6, 38, 40, 124–5, 142
Heidegger, Martin 35, 40, 101
Heraclitus 19
Herodotus 86
Herzl, Theodor 41
Homer 131, 132
Hosea 102, 104

illness 14, 95–9, 101, 103, 105, 106
Impressionism 76
Isaac 102
Isaiah 22, 48, 64, 96, 103, 110–11, 113–14

Jaspers, Karl 124
Jeremiah 23, 87
Jesus 64, 96, 112, 113
Job 102, 109
John 23
John XXIII (Pope) 81
Joll, James 80
Jonah 112
Josephus 141
Jouvenel, Bertrand de 63
Judaism 4, 5, 8, 18, 22, 37, 41, 85, 110
Jungk, Robert 61, 63

Kapp, Karl William 134
Kennedy, John F. 81
Kierkegaard, Søren 35
Kropotkin, Peter 75, 78–81

Landauer, Gustav 12, 79
language viii–ix, 21–2, 124
Lenin, Vladimir 36, 41, 81
love 20, 26, 74, 93, 94, 96–100, 103, 106, 120
Lüthy, Herbert 122
Luther, Martin 75

Mackay, John Henry 79
Makhno, Nestor Ivanovych 80
manipulation 13, 41, 53, 57, 59–62
Mao Zedong 36–9
Marcuse, Herbert 2, 3, 12, 13, 59, 74, 80–2

Marx, Karl 12, 23, 34–6, 40, 53, 74, 80–2, 108, 136
Mohammed 75

Nicholas of Cusa 29–30
Nietzsche, Friedrich 3, 69–70, 89–90, 101, 108
nihilism 3, 68–71, 73

Packard, Vance 60
Parmenides 19
Paul 27, 28, 87, 93, 102, 104, 108
Peter 26, 124–5
philosophy viii–ix, 1–7, 9, 11, 18–20, 22–5, 30, 33–7, 69–70, 77, 103, 105, 125, 127, 134
Pissarro, Camille 76
Plato 18, 19, 22–4, 33–4, 95
Popper, Karl Raimund 67
Portmann, Adolf 62
Prometheus 23
Proudhon, Pierre-Joseph 11, 73, 75–9, 81

reason 18–21, 25, 29, 34, 102, 103, 115
revelation 18, 29, 34, 115
rhetoric viii–ix, 12, 19

Scheler, Max 103
Schiller, Friedrich 56, 90
Schopenhauer, Arthur 33
science 2, 19, 20, 23, 39, 41, 43, 46, 47, 50, 60, 62, 66–70, 97–100, 104, 106, 107, 115, 124, 132, 134
Smith, Adam 136
Socrates 19, 22–3, 33
Spinoza, Baruch de 109
Stalin, Joseph 36
Stirner, Max 11–12, 73, 76–9, 81
sublation (*Aufhebung*) viii, 33–5, 121, 124–5, 139, 142
Sun Tzu 36

technology viii, 14, 40–8, 52, 60, 65, 78, 104, 106, 134
Thales of Miletus 19
theology 25, 30, 34, 35, 128
Toffler, Alvin 64
Tolstoy, Leo 11, 73–5, 78, 79–82

totalitarianism 13, 41, 43, 49, 51–3, 55, 57, 59–60, 67–8, 122
truth 2, 7, 18–20, 22–9, 32, 33–6, 49, 51, 68–9, 71, 76–9, 102, 104, 113, 114, 117–19
Turel, Adrien 44, 46, 64–5, 129
Turning (*teshuva*) 21–3, 60–4, 109–14

Vico, Giambattista 100

Weber, Max 19
Wei Chengi 36, 39
Wust, Peter 27, 28

Zarathustra 89–90
Zephaniah 115
Zeus 131

INDEX OF BIBLE PASSAGES

Reference	Page
Gen. 1:27	21
Gen. 1:28	43
Gen. 2:18	21
Gen. 2:20	21
Gen. 2:23	21
Gen. 3:17	22
Gen. 3:21	42
Gen. 4:3	21
Gen. 4:7	21
Gen. 4:9	21
Gen. 11:1–9	21
Gen. 12:1	22
Gen. 12:3	22
Gen. 25:8	102
Gen. 35:29	102
Exod. 20:2	87
Exod. 20:4	75
Exod. 21:2	87
Exod. 23:9	131
Lev. 19:18	26, 94, 120
Lev. 19:34	26
Lev. 25:4	131
Lev. 25:10	85
Lev. 25:23	131
Lev. 26:33	131
Lev. 26:34	131
Deut. 5:6	87
Deut. 5:8	75
Deut. 15:12	87
Deut. 15:14	87
2 Sam. 13:3	96
Isa. 2:4	23, 48
Isa. 2:10	64
Isa. 5:20	114
Isa. 6:9–11	23
Isa. 10:20–22	111
Isa. 11:11,16	111
Isa. 40:11	113
Isa. 53:3,4	96
Isa. 53:11	103
Isa. 58:5–7	96
Isa. 60:1	64
Isa. 61:1	64, 110
Jer. 27:12	23
Jer. 28:1	23
Jer. 34:8	87
Jer. 34:14	87
Jer. 34:17	88
Jer. 38:1	23
Ezek. 18:20–22	111
Ezek. 18:30–32	110
Ezek. 33:14–16	113
Ezek. 34:11,16	113
Hos. 13:14	102
Jonah 3:2,3,5,10	112
Mic. 4:3	48
Zeph. 3:15	115
Ps. 41:1,2,4	96
Ps. 73:12	109
Prov. 14:12	23
Prov. 16:25	23
Job 21:10–13	109
Job 42:17	102
Song 8:6–7	100
1 Chr. 29:28	102

Index of Bible passages

Ben Sira 33:15	28
Matt. 3:2	110
Matt. 4:17	110
Matt. 7:2	114
Matt. 12:39	112
Matt. 12:41	112
Matt. 16:4	112
Matt. 25:35–40	97
Luke 4:17	64
Luke 10:29	120
Luke 15:4–7	113
John 21:11	26
Rom. 7:15,19	108
Rom. 8:21	75
Rom. 11:18	108
Cor. 1 7:20–22	87
Cor. 1 15:28	23
Cor. 1 15:54–55	102
Cor. 1 15:56	104
Cor. 2 6:7	28
Gal. 5:13,14	93
1 John 4:1	23

www.ingramcontent.com/pod-product-compliance
Lightning Source LLC
Chambersburg PA
CBHW052050300426
44117CB00012B/2055